Pojo's Unofficial TC

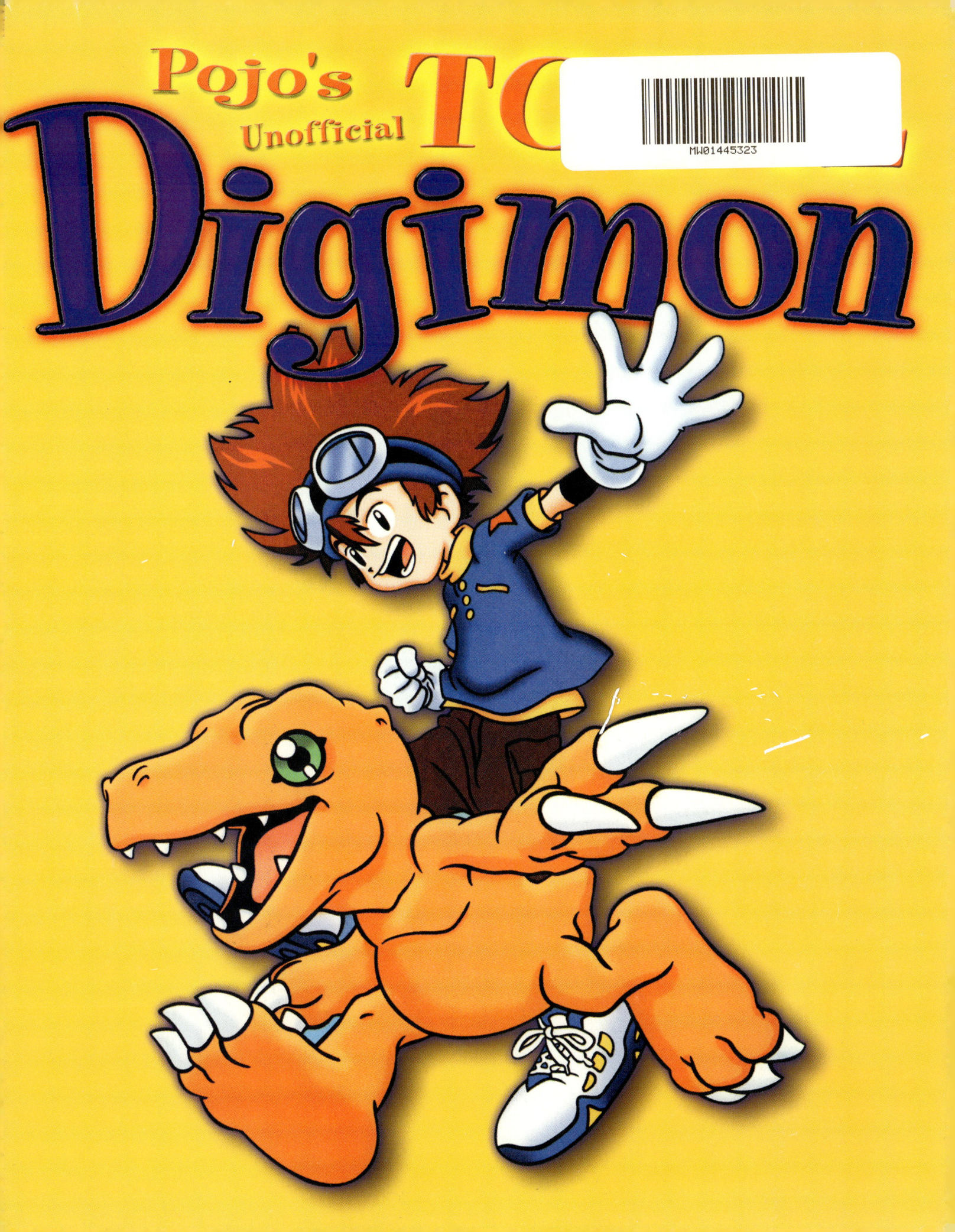

Digimon

© 2000 Contents H&S Media, Inc. All rights reserved.

DIGIMON, DIGITAL MONSTERS are trademarks of Bandai/Toei Animation.

UPPER DECK is a trademark of The Upper Deck Company, LLC.

Total Digimon is not sponsored or endorsed by, or otherwise affiliated with Bandai/Toei Animation or its licensees. Any opinions expressed are solely those of the authors, and do not necessarily reflect those of Bandai/Toei Animation.

No part of this publication may be reproduced, stored in a retrieval system, or transmitted, in any form by any means, electronic, mechanical, photocopying, or otherwise, without the prior written consent of the publisher, Triumph Books, 601 South LaSalle Street, Suite 500, Chicago, Illinois 60605.

Printed and bound in the United States of America

This book is available in quantity at special discounts for your group or organization. For more information, contact:

TRIUMPH BOOKS
601 South LaSalle Street
Suite 500
Chicago, Illinois 60605
(312)939-3330
Fax (312)663-3557

ISBN 1-57243-371-X

10 9 8 7 6 5 4 3 2

Pojo's Unofficial TOTAL Digimon

The Complete Player and Collector's Guide to every card and character

TRIUMPH BOOKS
601 South LaSalle Street
Chicago, Illinois 60605

Pojo's Unofficial TOTAL Digimon

6 Digi-News
What's happening in the world of Digimon.

8 Digi-Web
Check out the best Web sites devoted to Digimon.

10 Meet the Digimon
They're big, they're small, they shoot Pepper Breath at ya — who wouldn't love 'em?

28 A Digi-Destined TCG
The scoop on Upper Deck's Digimon trading-card game — and the Japanese games from which it has derived.

38 Pet the Digimon
The original Digimon toys still pack a wallop.

Digi contents

46 Daring Digital Adventures
A guided tour through the TV series' 54 breathtaking episodes.

58 Digimon... The Movie?
The stories behind the two films you've probably never seen.

68 Digi-Mall
Wear them, play with them, take them everywhere--the latest Digimon toys.

80 Can't Collect Just Digi-One
Better narrow your focus before you go gonzo.

87 Digimon Cards & Prices
What you need to know to start collecting.

109 Digi-Fun
Challenge yourself with fun Digimon puzzles.

Digi news

Flop 'N' Plop

Picture this: It's been a long, hard day. All you want to do is head to your room, shut the door and plop down onto an inflatable Digimon chair and watch the latest episode of *Digimon Adventures*.

A pipe dream? No way — now that Kidz Kraze has come out with its line of Digimon inflatable furniture. The Digimon furniture gives you a three-dimensional Digimon experience as well as a place to flop your tired bones. Products like night-lights, bedside lights, switchplates, flashlights and squeeze lights will complement the inflatables. Kidz Kraze products are available at FAO Schwarz, Wal-Mart, Toys "R" Us, Kay-Bee Toys, Kmart, Target and Sears. For more information, call Kidz Kraze at (516) 931-3600.

Only 250 Shopping Days Left

You'll be seeing the latest batch of Bandai's Digimon products in this magazine — but that's just the tip of Bandai's Digimon iceberg. The real rush comes around Christmas, when Bandai will be rolling with:
• Twelve 2.5-inch Digimon action figures
• Nine bean plush (Agumon, Biyomon, Gabumon, Gomamon, Palmon, Patamon, Tentomon, Sunomon and Koromon)
• Four deluxe plush characters (Garurumon, Ikkakumon, Togemon and Greymon)
• Three Talking Digimon figures (Agumon, Gabumon and Patamon)
• Two 5-inch Digivolving action figures (Metal Greymon and WereGarurumon)
• One micro playset, which includes one character and one Digivolving Digimon
• One sticker series
• One Digimon backpack

Sweet-Smelling Rose

Like to draw Digimon? Even if you don't, crayon-and-craft company Rose Art has a bunch of fun Digimon stuff for you coming this summer.

The fun starts with a Digimon Super Draw, a Magnadoodle-like drawing slate with an attached stylus. You can sketch out a quick Palmon on the slate, and if you don't like it, wipe the slate clean with no one being the wiser.

Next comes a figure maker with modeling compound and molds. At press time, Rose Art didn't know if the modeling compound would be closer to Play-Doh or clay, but a compound of either type will be pressed into molds shaped like your favorite Digimon and even a few of the kids. An adventure playset rounds out Rose Art's summer Digimon offerings.

It doesn't stop there. Rose Art subsidiary Warren also will be doing the Digimon this summer. Among its products are a series of 50-piece mini-puzzles and 100-plus-piece, non-mini-puzzles featuring scenes from the animated series; 100-plus-piece puzzle clocks, which when assembled form a picture of all the Rookie Digimon and their kids; and activity packs with special removable stickers.

Rose Art and Warren products will be available at mass retailers across the country.

Digimon Spring

It looks like a Digimon spring. Shipments of Pentech's Digimon-brand pencils and pens will begin this month, in plenty of time to capture back-to-school and holiday 2000 sales. All4Fun (part of the Canadian company that brought Crazy Bones to North America) has a series of Digimon coins ready to roll. Also, Digimon

All4Fun's Digimon coi[ns] are beginni[ng] to spring u[p]

www.brownshoe.com, www.pentechintl.com and www.all4funtoys.com.

New Kids on the Block

Just when you thought you had the Digiworld down pat, here comes a totally revised Digiworld. The second generation of *Digimon Adventures,* titled, appropriately enough, *Digimon Adventures 02,* premiered in Japan earlier this spring.

Details on *Digimon Adventures 02* are sketchy, but it appears that the series takes place three years after the Digi-Destined first entered the Digiworld. This time around, the old kids are T.K. and Kari, joined by Daisuke, Miyako and Iori. All the kids have Rookie and Champion Digimon — including their evil classmate, Satoru.

Unlike what happened when Dragonball changed into Dragonball Z, the shift from *Digimon Adventures* to *Digimon Adventures 02* doesn't seem to involve huge changes in characters or their missions. The kids are still kids, the Digimon are still Digimon, and the main battle is between good and evil.

There's no timetable for getting *Digimon Adventures 02* onto U.S. TV, but based on Digimon's popularity, it's more likely to happen sooner rather than later.

Look for more information on *Digimon Adventures 02* at www.pojo.com as it becomes available. *Digimon*

Bandai America CEO Brian Goldner greets Agumon and Bigomon at FAO Schwarz in New York.

Digimon Adventures 02 takes place three years after the original.

athletic shoes and rugged play sandals from Brown Shoe's Pagoda line will be available in major mass-merchandise stores starting this spring.

"We expect these shoes to be a monster of a brand, since the characters are hot and appeal to Buster Brown & Company's consumers — young children ages 3 to 7," said Gary Rich, president of Brown's Pagoda division. "Kids want character shoes like Digimon. And, that use of popular cartoon characters ignites kids' development to learn how to put on and tie (or Velcro-close) their own shoes. This, coupled with their affordable price, is one reason parents buy them for their kids."

For more information on these and other products, check out the various company Web sites:

Digiweb

Web surfers, browsers and electronic media fanatics everywhere, listen up! Digimania is flying high, and there's no better way to catch the wave than through the ever-evolving world of cyberspace. The primo Web sites listed here are the best way to keep up with gaming tips, collector trends, new merchandise or anything else that comprises the great wide Digiworld.

Upper Deck
www.upperdeck.com

Digivolve. Digibattle. View quicktime movies. Reference strategy tips and game-play instructions. And beginners, don't forget to check out the FAQ section. It should answer all your questions and put you on the fast track to full-fledged Digimania.

Gordon Kane's Digimon Museum
www.geocities.com/bigdigimon

Better be in site-seeing mode when you step inside this museum; a complete tour could take a while. You'll quickly find it's worth your time, however, as it's neatly divided into eight major categories: Media, Technology, Xenobiology, Competition, Statuary, Future Attractions, Souvenir Shop and Information Center. Each category is loaded with useful (and fun) information, from Digimon movie facts to full-size views of cards.

Fox Kids
www.foxkids.com/digimon

How can you visit the Fox Kids home page without checking out the Video Zone? You can't. As expected, the Zone is the crown jewel of the Digimon portion of the site. To enter, simply click Real Player or Windows Media Player, grab some popcorn and a soda, stretch out on your favorite recliner, and watch the Digishow unfold!

Bandai
www.bandai.com/dm

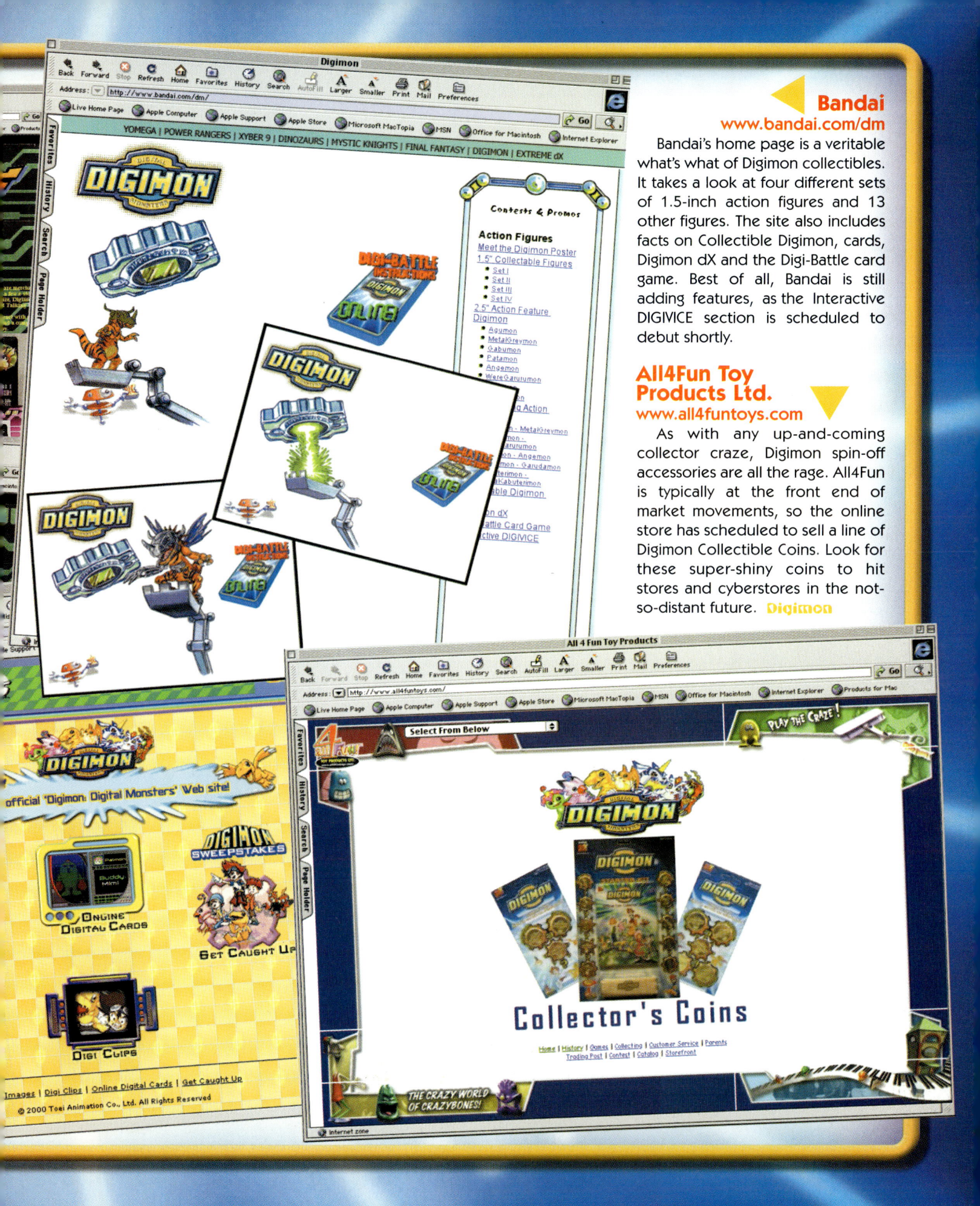

Bandai's home page is a veritable what's what of Digimon collectibles. It takes a look at four different sets of 1.5-inch action figures and 13 other figures. The site also includes facts on Collectible Digimon, cards, Digimon dX and the Digi-Battle card game. Best of all, Bandai is still adding features, as the Interactive DIGIVICE section is scheduled to debut shortly.

All4Fun Toy Products Ltd.
www.all4funtoys.com

As with any up-and-coming collector craze, Digimon spin-off accessories are all the rage. All4Fun is typically at the front end of market movements, so the online store has scheduled to sell a line of Digimon Collectible Coins. Look for these super-shiny coins to hit stores and cyberstores in the not-so-distant future. **Digimon**

Meet the Digimon

Tai Kamiya
(Yagami Taichi)

Tai's the leader of the Chosen Kids, but that doesn't always mean he can be counted on to do the right thing. Tai's a born leader and super-aggressive — usually the first to spring into action — but he doesn't always think before he acts. The results often spell danger for all the kids. His little sister, Hikari, is also one of the Chosen Children. Back in the real world, he's an 11-year-old fifth-grader at (the Japanese) Odaiba Elementary School. Naturally, his crest is Courage.

They're big, they're small, they shoot Pepper Breath at ya — who wouldn't love 'em?

By Gordon Kane and Kit Kiefer

Seven kids at summer camp are suddenly and mysteriously transported to File Island, a strange digital world that's seemingly a million miles away from their real homes and families. Soon after their arrival, each kid is befriended by a Digimon, one of the many digital monsters that roams this odd world. Soon the team-ups form: Tai and Koromon. Izzy and Motimon. Sora and Yocomon. T.K. and Tokomon. Matt and Tsunomon. Joe and Bukamon. Mimi and Tanemon.

Later, the Digimon start to evolve. Koromon becomes Agumon. Yocomon becomes Biyomon. Motimon becomes Tentomon...

The kids and their Digimon bond quickly, and the little creatures band together to protect their human friends. They each have the ability to transform into giant Champion Digimon to fight other giant Digimon who want to harm the kids.

It's a strange world full of strange characters, all right. And if you want to make a little sense of it all, you need to know who's bad, who's good…and who's who. Here's your guide.

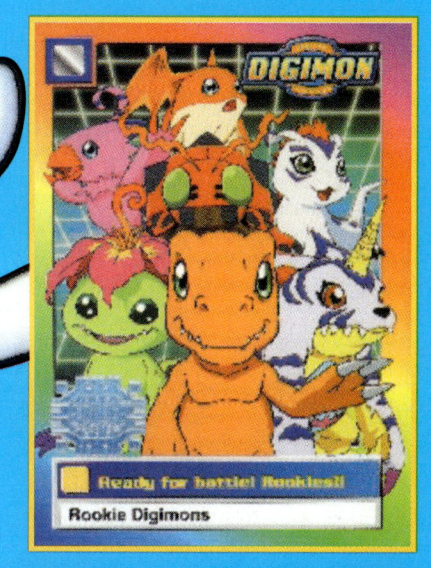

Koromon

Your basic legless pink pig with teeth.

Type: Unclassified
Classification: Micro Digimon
Stage: In-Training
Technique: Bubble-Blow
Size: 10 G
Evolutions: Agumon, Greymon, MetalGreymon, WereGreymon

Agumon

Everyone's favorite li'l dinosaur. Watch out, though — that Pepper Breath's a killer.

Type: Vaccine
Classification: Reptile Digimon
Stage: Child/Rookie
Japanese Attack: Baby Flame
U.S. Technique: Pepper Breath
Evolves From: Koromon
Evolutions: Greymon, WereGreymon, MetalGreymon

Greymon

It's a major step forward from Pepper Breath to Nova Blast.

Type: Vaccine
Classification: Dinosaur Digimon
Stage: Champion
Technique: Nova Blast
Size: 30 G
Evolves From: Agumon
Evolutions: WereGreymon, MetalGreymon

WereGreymon

A bigger, tougher, more powerful Greymon, but no match for MetalGreymon.

Type: Vaccine
Stage: Ultimate
Evolves From: Greymon
Evolutions: MetalGreymon

MetalGreymon

The ultimate cyborg form of Greymon.

Type: Vaccine
Stage: Mega
Evolves From: WereGreymon

Digimon 11

Meet the Digimon

Sora Takenouchi
(Takenouchi Sora)

Sora's down-to-earth maturity contrasts with Tai's rambunctious love of adventure. She's a tomboy whose first duty in the DigiWorld is keeping the other kids safe. She's not always sure Tai can handle the situation…but who is? Back in the real world, she's an 11-year-old fifth-grader at Odaiba Elementary and plays on the soccer team with Tai and Koushirou.

Yokomon

Just the sort of thing you'd want to brighten up that drab corner of the house.

Type: Unclassified
Classification: Micro Digimon
Stage: In-Training
Technique: Bubble Blow
Size: 4 G
Evolutions: Biyomon, Birdramon, Garudamon

Biyomon

Much more Pidgeot than Moltres.

Type: Vaccine
Classification: Bird Digimon
Stage: Rookie/Child
Japanese Attack: Magical Fire
U.S. Technique: Spiral Twister
Evolves From: Pyokomon/Yokomon
Evolutions: Birdramon, Garudamon

Birdramon

Much more Moltres than Pidgeot.

Type: Vaccine
Classification: Bird Digimon
Stage: Champion
Technique: MeteorWing
Size: 30 G
Evolves From: Biyomon
Evolutions: Garudamon

Garudamon

A bigger, tougher, more powerful Birdramon — about what you'd expect.

Type: Vaccine
Stage: Ultimate
Evolves From: Birdramon

Meet the Digimon

Matt Ishida
(Yumato Ishida)

Rebellious, quiet and aloof, Matt wants to do things his own way and isn't keen on other people's suggestions. That's led to plenty of clashes with Tai, and while he's lost his share of battles, he can always be counted on for a joke when times are tough. He's cool, all right, but he really loves his little brother, T.K. In the real world, he's an 11-year-old fifth-grader at Odaiba Elementary. He carries the Friendship crest.

Tsunomon

Chip (of Chip 'n' Dale) with a big fin sticking out of his head and no legs.

Type: Unclassified
Classification: Micro Digimon
Stage: In-Training
Technique: Bubble Blow
Size: 10 G
Evolutions: Gabumon, Garurumon, WereGarurumon, MetalGarurumon

Gabumon

A weird color scheme obscures a darn nice monster.

Type: Data
Classification: Reptile Digimon
Stage: Child/Rookie
Japanese Attack: Petit Fire
U.S. Technique: Blue Blaster
Size: 20 G
Evolves From: Tsunomon
Evolutions: Garurumon, WereGarurumon, Metal Garurumon

Garurumon

A tough, heroic wolf monster with a siren-like attack.

Type: Data
Classification: Animal Digimon
Stage: Champion
Technique: Howling Blaster
Size: 20 G
Evolves From: Gabumon
Evolutions: WereGarurumon, MetalGarurumon

WereGarurumon

A pumped-up werewolf version of Garurumon.

Type: Data
Stage: Ultimate
Evolves From: Garurumon
Evolutions: Metal Garurumon

MetalGarurumon

A semi-cyborg version of WereGarurumon.

Type: Data
Stage: Mega
Evolves From: Garurumon

This magazine is not sponsored by Akiyoshi Hongo Toei Animation, Bandai, or The Upper Deck Company, LLC. DIGIMON, DIGITAL MONSTERS and all related logos, names and distinctive likenesses thereof are the property of Bandai/Toei Animation.

Digimon 15

Meet the Digimon

Joe Kido
(Kido Jou)

Remember the story of Chicken Little, who always ran around proclaiming that the sky is falling? That's Joe. He's a pessimist and a hypochondriac and so much more; he's convinced that if anything can go wrong it will. In fact, he worries so much that he almost throws himself into panic time after time. And here's the scary part: Many times he's right. Joe's worrying comes from a good place, too. Since he's the oldest — he's a 12-year-old sixth-grader — he feels responsible and wants to protect the others. Joe's crest is Honesty.

Bukamon/Pukamon

A legless Charmander with a flame issuing from his skull.

Type: Unclassified
Classification: Micro Digimon
Stage: In-Training
Technique: Bubble Blow
Size: 7 G
Evolutions: Gomamon, Ikkakumon, Zudomon

Gomamon

Half sea lion, half real lion, half polar bear. Three halves? This guy can handle that.

Type: Vaccine
Classification: Water/Sea Animal Digimon
Stage: Child/Rookie
Japanese Attack: Marching Fishes
U.S. Technique: Marching Fishes
Size: 15 G
Evolves From: Pukamon/Bukamon
Evolutions: Ikkakumon, Zudomon

Ikkakumon

Half sheepdog but all walrus.

Type: Vaccine
Classification: Water/Sea Animal Digimon
Stage: Champion
Technique: Harpoon Torpedo
Size: 25 G
Evolves From: Gomamon
Evolutions: Zudomon

Zudomon

A turtle-like creature with a killer knockout punch.

Type: Vaccine
Stage: Ultimate
Evolves From: Ikkakumon

Meet the Digimon

Mimi Tachikawa
(Tachikawa Mimi)

Mimi has a lot to learn about the ways of the DigiWorld. A sheltered and slightly spoiled child in the real world, "Daddy's little princess" sometimes has trouble adapting to her new surroundings. She shows her incompatibility with her new surroundings by whining and refusing to help out. She's not selfish; she's actually quite sweet. She just has trouble understanding what's going on around her. Back home she's a 10-year-old fourth-grader. Her crest is Purity.

Tanemon

Bean-sprout monster.

Type: Unclassified
Classification: Micro Digimon
Stage: In-Training
Technique: Bubble Blow
Size: 10 G
Evolutions: Palmon, Togemon, Lilymon

Palmon

An orchid with teeth.

Type: Data
Classification: Plant Digimon
Stage: Child/Rookie
Japanese Attack: Poison Ivy
U.S. Technique: Poison Ivy
Size: 15 G
Evolves From: Tanemon
Evolutions: Togemon, Lilymon

Togemon

A cactus with a killer uppercut.

Type: Data
Classification: Plant/Vegetation Digimon
Stage: Champion
Technique: Needle Spray
Size: 20 G
Evolves From: Palmon
Evolutions: Lilymon

Lilymon

A killer pixie, if that makes any sense. Think Tinker Bell, only huge.

Type: Data
Stage: Ultimate
Evolves From: Togemon

Meet the Digimon

T.K. Takaishi
(Takaisha Takeru)

T.K. really wants to be brave because he doesn't want the others to know he's afraid, and he wants to impress big brother Matt. But it's hard sometimes. T.K. is thrilled to be spending so much time with Matt. Their parents are divorced and they don't live together anymore, so T.K. doesn't get to see Matt that often. T.K.'s the youngest member of the group — an 8-year-old second grader at Kawada Elementary in real life — and a real sweet-natured and generous kid. He does what you ask him to but he's a bit of a crybaby. He carries the Hope crest.

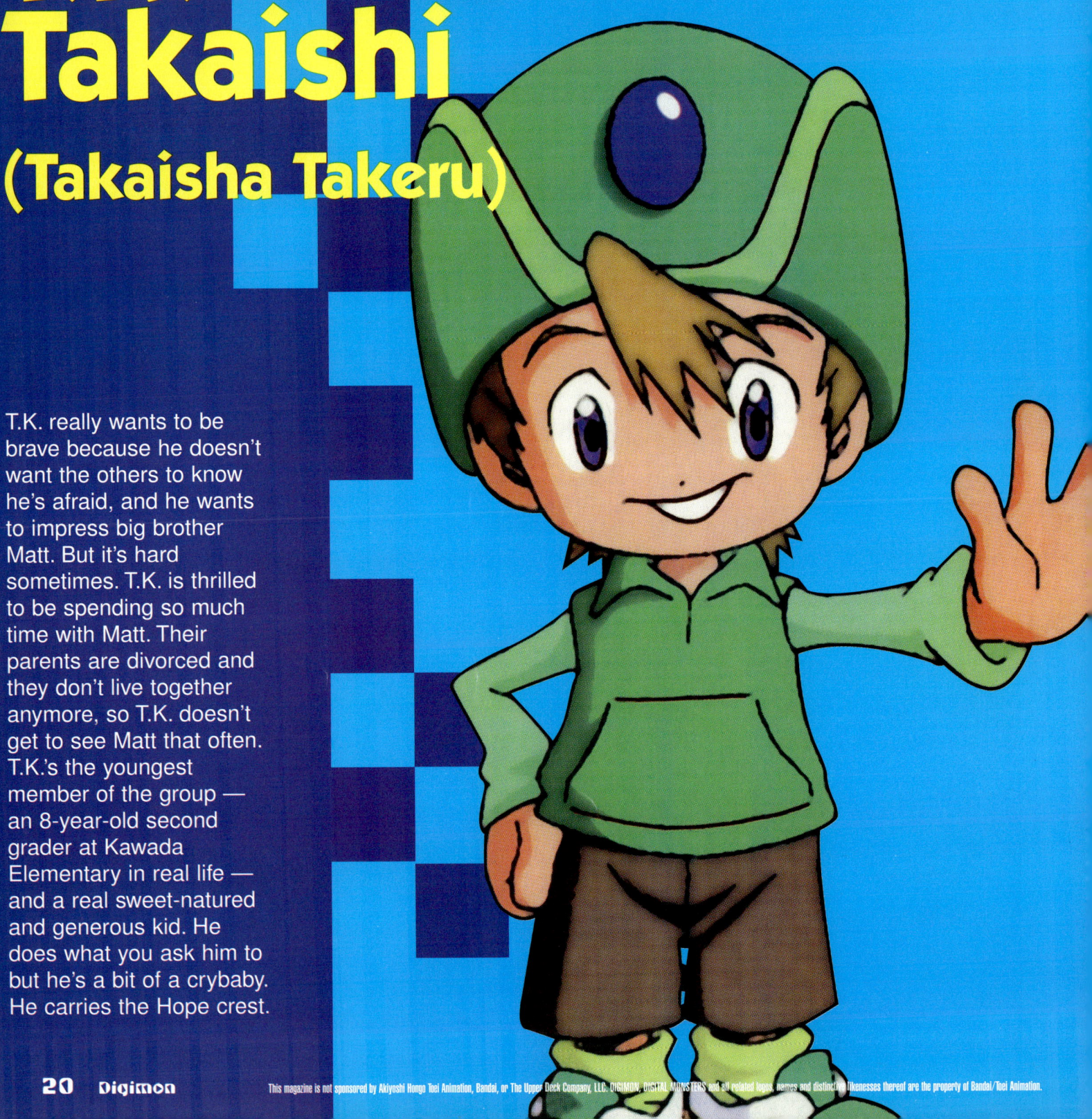

Tokomon

Highly, highly sweet.

Type: Unclassified
Classification: Micro
Stage: In Training
Technique: Bubble Blow
Size: 10 G
Evolutions: Patamon, Angemon

Patamon

Big-eared Pikachu. All the cries of "Pokémon ripoff!" start here.

Type: Data
Classification: Mammal Digimon
Stage: Child/Rookie
Japanese Attack: Air Shot
U.S. Technique: Boom Bubble
Size: 20 G
Evolves From: Tokomon
Evolutions: Angemon

Angemon

Major digivolutionary jump; one of the show's favorite (and best) characters.

Type: Vaccine
Classification: Angel Digimon
Stage: Champion
Technique: Hand of Fate
Size: 20 G
Evolves From: Patamon

Meet the Digimon

Izzy Izumi
(Izumi Koushirou)

The ultimate computer whiz, Izzy spends all his time trying to figure stuff out on his Pineapple laptop. He has a theory about everything — including why he's adopted (or so he thinks). You'd think that with his brain and his love of computers, the Digiworld would be the perfect place for him, but Izzy gets so wrapped up in his own thoughts and projects that he doesn't see the danger around him. He's a 10-year-old fourth-grader at Odaiba, and naturally, he carries the Knowledge crest.

Motimon

Bubble-gum-bubble Digimon.

Type: Unclassified
Classification: Micro Digimon
Stage: In-Training
Technique: Bubble-Blow
Size: 8 G
Evolutions: Tentamon, Kabuterimon, MegaKabuterimon

Tentamon

Scarab-beetle Digimon.

Type: Vaccine
Classification: Insect Digimon
Stage: Child/Rookie
Japanese Attack: Petit Thunder
U.S. Technique: Super Shocker
Size: 15 G
Evolves From: Motimon
Evolutions: Kabuterimon, MegaKabuterimon

Kabuterimon

Aren't you glad he's a good guy?

Type: Vaccine
Classification: Insect Digimon
Stage: Champion
Technique: Electro Shocker
Size: 30 G
Evolves From: Tentomon
Evolutions: MegaKabuterimon

MetalKabuterimon

A big insect. A very big insect.

Type: Vaccine
Stage: Mega Digimon
Evolves From: Kabuterimon

This magazine is not sponsored by Akiyoshi Hongo Toei Animation, Bandai, or The Upper Deck Company, LLC. DIGIMON, DIGITAL MONSTERS and all related logos, names and distinctive likenesses thereof are the property of Bandai/Toei Animation.

Meet the Digimon

Meramon

Leomon

The New Kids
These kids appeared in the new *Digimon Adventures 02* anime, which hasn't yet been seen in North America.

Daisuke
Daisuke has one Rookie Digimon and two Champion Digimon. Buimon is his Rookie, and his Champions are Raidramon, a four-legged black/blue creature with a jagged horn/blade, and Freidramon, a two-legged creature with flames on its armor.

Miyako
Miyako's Rookie Digimon is Hawkmon, a red bird with an Indian headband. Her co-champions are Horusmon, a four-legged cross between an eagle and a lion, and Shurimon, a two-legged creature with a veil over its face.

Hikari/Kari
Hikari/Kari is Tai's sister. Her Digimon include Nyaromon, a cuddly kitty Digimon with ears and a tail; a dog-like Salamon; Gatomon, a much meaner breed of cat; Angewomon and Neferatimon, a curious four-legged creature that looks like the Sphinx, but with a feminine face.

Iori
Iori is the new young one, taking over from T.K. Armadimon is his Rookie, and as you might guess from his name, he looks like an armadillo. His co-champions are the shark-like Submarimon, and the two-legged Digmon, with powerful drill cones on its face and hands.

Satoru
The evil human from the new series of shows. His Rookie is the equally evil Wormmon.

Other Characters
Gennai
Gennai is the typical wise old guy who appears in just about every anime cartoon. In this case, he takes form in a beam of light and knows about the DigiWorld and the real world.

SkullGreymon
This creature appeared after Tai got force-fed Agumon. Agumon evolved into Greymon and then SkullGreymon, who can't tell good from evil.

Wizardmon
Wizardmon has spent time on the good and bad sides. He and Gatomon wound up in Myotismon's army, but died helping Gatomon find her identity and place in the DigiWorld.

Other Vaccine/Data Digimon
Cockatrimon
Type: Data
Classification: Bird Digimon
Stage: Champion
Technique: Frozen Fire Shot
Size: 20 G

Frigimon
Type: Vaccine
Classification: Icy Digimon
Stage: Champion
Technique: Subzero Ice Punch
Size: 30 G

Leomon
Leomon (yes, just like it sounds — a lion Digimon) is a strong, good digimon who turned bad when he was possessed by the Black Gears.
Type: Vaccine
Classification: Animal Digimon
Stage: Champion
Technique: Fist of the Beat King
Size: 20 G

Seadramon
Type: Data
Classification: Sea Animal Digimon
Stage: Champion
Technique: Ice Blast
Size: 20 G

Meramon
Type: Data
Classification: Fire Digimon
Stage: Champion
Technique: Fireball
Size: 18 G

Monochromon
Type: Data
Classification: Dinosaur Digimon
Stage: Champion
Technique: Volcano Strike
Size: 30 G

Evil (Virus) Digimon
Kuwagemon
Type: Virus
Classification: Insectoid Digimon
Stage: Champion
Technique: Scissor-Claw
Size: 20 G →

The New Kids

Ogremon
Ogremon's one shot at glory was in the big showdown between Devimon and Angemon.
Type: Virus
Classification: Evil Digimon
Stage: Champion
Technique: Pummel Whack
Size: 20

Devimon
Devimon controlled the Black Gears until he was defeated by Angemon.
Type: Virus
Classification: Evil Digimon
Stage: Champion
Technique: Touch of Evil
Size: 15 G

Bakemon
Type: Virus
Classification: Ghost Digimon
Stage: Champion
Technique: Dark Claw
Size: 30 G

Etemon
Old-time rock-'n'-roll legend Etemon is the kingpin of the continent of Server. He's shaped like a monkey and talks like Elvis and actually has his own songs — or did, until MetalGreymon took him down.

Gazimon
Etemon's creepy little underlings.

Myotismon
A vampire Digimon, and the current bad guy.

DemiDevimon
Myotismon's creepy little underling.

Unclassified Digimon (Japanese names)

Name	Type	Appeared
Botamon	Fresh	DigiMon 1
Punimon	Fresh	DigiMon 2
Poyomon	Fresh	DigiMon 3
Yuramon	Fresh	DigiMon 4
Zurumon	Fresh	DigiMon 5
Pugmon	In Training	DigiMon 5
Babumon	Fresh	Pendulum 1
Mochimon	In Training	Pendulum 1
Pitchmon	Fresh	Pendulum 2
Mokumon	Fresh	Pendulum 3
Petite Meramon	In Training	Pendulum 3
Nyokimon	Fresh	Pendulum 4
Pyokomon	In Training	Pendulum 4
Choromon	Fresh	Pendulum 5
Kapurimon	In Training	Pendulum 5

Virus Digimon (Japanese names)

Name	Type	Appeared
Betamon	Rookie	DigiMon 1
Devimon	Champion	DigiMon 1, Pendulum 3
Numemon	Champion	DigiMon 1
Vegiemon	Champion	DigiMon 2
SkullGreymon	Ultimate	DigiMon 2
Vademon	Ultimate	DigiMon 2
Kunemon	Rookie	DigiMon 3
Ogremon	Champion	DigiMon 3
Bakemon	Champion	DigiMon 3, Pendulum 3
Sukamon	Champion	DigiMon 3
Etemon	Ultimate	DigiMon 3
Kuwagamon	Champion	DigiMon 4, Pendulum 1
Nanimon	Ultimate	DigiMon 4
Megadramon	Ultimate	DigiMon 4
Gazimon	Rookie	DigiMon 5
Gizamon	Rookie	DigiMon 5
Dark Tyranomon	Champion	DigiMon 5
Cyclomon	Champion	DigiMon 5
Devidramon	Champion	DigiMon 5
Tuskmon	Champion	DigiMon 5
Flymon	Champion	DigiMon 5
Deltamon	Champion	DigiMon 5
Raremon	Champion	DigiMon 5
Metal Tyranomon	Ultimate	DigiMon 5
Datamon	Ultimate	DigiMon 5
X Tyranomon	Ultimate	DigiMon 5
Otamamon	Rookie	Pendulum 1
Tortamon	Champion	Pendulum 1
Gekomon	Champion	Pendulum 1
Okuwamon	Ultimate	Pendulum 1
ShogunGekomon	Ultimate	Pendulum 1
Metal Etemon	Mega	Pendulum 1
Shakomon	Rookie	Pendulum 2
Gesomon	Champion	Pendulum 2
Octmon	Champion	Pendulum 2
Marine Devimon	Ultimate	Pendulum 2
Dagomon	Ultimate	Pendulum 2
Pukumon	Mega	Pendulum 2
Demi Devimon	Rookie	Pendulum 3
Myotismon (VamDemon)	Ultimate	Pendulum 3
Phantomon	Ultimate	Pendulum 3
Piedmon	Mega	Pendulum 3
Woodmon	Champion	Pendulum 4
Red Vegiemon	Champion	Pendulum 3
Jyuremon	Ultimate	Pendulum 4
Garbagemon	Ultimate	Pendulum 4
Puppetmon	Mega	Pendulum 4
Kokuwamon	Rookie	Pendulum 5
Guardmon	Champion	Pendulum 5
Mechanimon	Champion	Pendulum 5
Metal Dramon	Ultimate	Pendulum 5
WereMonzaemon	Ultimate	Pendulum 5
MachineDramon	Mega	Pendulum 5

Vaccine Digimon (Japanese names)

Name	Type	Appeared
Agumon	Rookie	DigiMon 1, Digivice
Greymon	Champion	DigiMon 1, Pendulum 5, Digivice
Airdramon	Champion	DigiMon 1
MetalGreymon	Ultimate	DigiMon 1, Pendulum 5, Digivice
Monzaemon	Ultimate	DigiMon 1
Kabuterimon	Champion	DigiMon 2, Pendulum 1
Angemon	Champion	DigiMon 2
Frigimon	Champion	DigiMon 2
Whamon	Champion	DigiMon 2, Pendulum 2
Unimon	Champion	DigiMon 3
Andromon	Ultimate	DigiMon 3, Pendulum 5
Giromon	Ultimate	DigiMon 3
Biyomon	Rookie	DigiMon 4, Pendulum 4
Birdramon	Champion	DigiMon 4
Mojamon	Champion	DigiMon 4
Tentomon	Rookie	Pendulum 1
MegaKabuterimon	Ultimate	Pendulum 1
Jagamon	Ultimate	Pendulum 1
Hercules Kabuterimon	Mega	Pendulum 1
Gomamon	Rookie	Pendulum 2
Ikkakumon	Champion	Pendulum 2
Rukamon (Dolphmon)	Champion	Pendulum 2
Zudomon	Ultimate	Pendulum 2
Marine Angemon	Mega	Pendulum 2
Bakumon (Tapirmon)	Rookie	Pendulum 3
Hanumon (Apemon)	Champion	Pendulum 3
Mammothmon	Ultimate	Pendulum 3
Skull Mammothmon	Mega	Pendulum 3
V Dramon	Champion	Pendulum 4
Aero V Dramon	Ultimate	Pendulum 4
Garudamon	Ultimate	Pendulum 4
Hououmon	Mega	Pendulum 4
Toy Agumon	Rookie	Pendulum 5
Robotmon	Champion	Pendulum 5
War Greymon	Mega	Pendulum 5

Data Digimon (Japanese names)

Name	Type	Appeared
Tyranomon	Champion	DigiMon 1
Meramon	Champion	DigiMon 1, Pendulum 3

Meet the Digimon

Name	Level	Source
Seadramon	Champion	DigiMon 1, Pendulum 2
Mamemon	Ultimate	DigiMon 1
Gabumon	Rookie	DigiMon 2
Elecmon	Rookie	DigiMon 2
Garurumon	Champion	DigiMon 2, Pendulum 3
Metal Mamemon	Ultimate	DigiMon 2
Patamon	Rookie	DigiMon 3
Centarumon	Champion	DigiMon 3
Shellmon	Champion	DigiMon 3
Drimogemon	Champion	DigiMon 3
WereGarurumon	Ultimate	Pendulum 3
Palmon	Rookie	DigiMon 4
Monochromon	Champion	DigiMon 4
Kokatorimon	Champion	DigiMon 4
Seelamon	Champion	DigiMon 4, Pendulum 2
Piximon	Ultimate	DigiMon 4, Pendulum 1
Digitamamon	Ultimate	DigiMon 4
Gotsumon	Rookie	Pendulum 1
Monochromon	Champion	Pendulum 1
Starmon	Champion	Pendulum 1
Triceramon	Ultimate	Pendulum 1
Saber Leomon	Mega	Pendulum 1
Ganimon (Crabmon)	Rookie	Pendulum 2
MegaSeadramon	Ultimate	Pendulum 2
Animal Okarimon	Ultimate	Pendulum 2
Metal Seadramon	Mega	Pendulum 2
Candlemon	Rookie	Pendulum 3
Wizardmon	Champion	Pendulum 3
Death Meramon (Skull Meramon)	Ultimate	Pendulum 3
Pumpkinmon	Ultimate	Pendulum 3
Brutemon (Boltmon)	Mega	Pendulum 3
Floramon	Rookie	Pendulum 4
Mushmon	Rookie	Pendulum 4
Togemon	Champion	Pendulum 4
Kiwimon	Champion	Pendulum 4
Blossomon	Ultimate	Pendulum 4
Delamon	Ultimate	Pendulum 4
Griffonmon	Mega	Pendulum 4
Gearmon	Rookie	Pendulum 5
Ganimon (Crabmon)	Rookie	Pendulum 2
Tankmon	Champion	Pendulum 5
Clockmon	Champion	Pendulum 5
Knightmon	Ultimate	Pendulum 5
Big Mamemon	Ultimate	Pendulum 5
Metal Garurmon	Mega	Pendulum 5

Devimon

Bakemon

Monochromon

Gabumon

Subscribe Today!

PoJo's Unofficial POKÉMON News & Price Guide Monthly
www.pojo.com

The Hottest Pokémon Magazine You Can Find!!!

INSIDE! Stadium Survival Tips!

PoJo's Unofficial POKÉMON News & Price Guide Monthly — Ultimate Strategy Guide

We also give you Pokémon game-playing strategies, and the latest information on video games and Web sites.

Get an in-depth look at the biggest craze going — Pokémon. See loads of full-color photos and price guides for all Pokémon trading cards.

Detach Here

Your Pokémon Source

Sign me up for my one-year subscription to **PoJo's Unofficial Pokémon News & Price Guide Monthly**

Only $49.95 for 12 HUGE ISSUES.

That's a 30% savings off the newsstand rate!

Name _____
Address _____
City _____
State _____ Zip _____ Phone (___)_____

G00106

Canadian Rate: $79.95 • Foreign Rate: $97.95 • U.S. funds only.

Payment Method: ☐ Check ☐ Money Order ☐ Visa ☐ MasterCard ☐ Bill Me
Card # _____ Exp. Date _____

Please allow 6 to 8 weeks for delivery of first issue. This magazine is not sponsored or endorsed by Nintendo of America, Inc. or Wizards of the Coast, Inc. Nintendo, Creatures, GAMEFREAK, Pokémon, Game Boy, Gotta catch 'em all!, and the official Nintendo seal are trademarks of Nintendo.

Mail To: *PoJo's Unofficial Pokémon News and Price Guide,* P.O. Box 500, Missouri City, TX 77459... or Fax To: 281-261-5999... or Call 1-800-310-7047 (9a.m.-5p.m. Central)

Digimon Special Feature
Game Overview

The Digi-Bat Card Game:
More than your average Poké-clone

By Gordon Kane

WHILE CRUISING THE AISLES AT TOYS "R" Us in early February looking for my next Digimon toy conquest, what should I find staring back at me but Upper Deck's Digimon Digi-Battle Card Game.

This was a bit strange for several reasons, not the least being that first-edition cards were supposed to be hobby-only (a reward to all those stores that, unlike Toys "R" Us and Kay-Bee Toys, make space for collectible card game (CCG) players to compete).

Since then, I've been learning about the North American game and comparing it to the Japanese starter sets and boosters available on eBay, Japanime.com and other online retailers.

Starter Decks

There are some big differences: The Japanese starter deck contains 38 of the initial set's 60 cards (numbered ST-1 through ST-60). It has three gold-embossed cards (WereGarurumon, Saber Leomon and Kimeramon) and three rainbow-foil cards (Pukumon, Metal Greymon Trainer and Hercules Kabuterimon). To get all 60 cards, you have to buy at least three starter decks and hope you get the three different card assortments. It's a very un-Japanese marketing ploy, more like one an American company would use.

A U.S. starter deck (left) contains 62 cards, while a Japanese one (right) has a mere 38.

The English starter, in contrast, contains 62 cards, used to create two decks that are played against each other. The problem is that a few of the cards that end up in Player One's deck may be necessary Digivolve characters in Player Two's deck (or vice-versa), while other cards can be found only in booster packs.

Booster Packs

U.S. booster-pack distribution also varies from the Japanese method. In Japan, Digi-Battle booster cards are available only in coin-operated vending machines. Each packet contains four cards from one of the three 54-card booster sets released to date. In the English-language series, the booster cards (numbered BO-1 through BO-54) are available in the familiar crimped-end Mylar packages, with eight cards per pack.

Oddly, not all cards are the same in the English and Japanese starter decks. For instance, the embossed cards in the Japanese series are not embossed (or otherwise differentiated) in the English series. The embossed Japanese Saber Leomon is an English rainbow-foil Saber Leomon, and the Japanese rainbow-foil Pukumon is just a normal card in the English series.

Cards ST-59 and ST-60 in the Japanese series are replaced by the English Red and Green/Yellow Digivice cards, and English cards ST-61 and ST-62 (which are cards in the Japanese Starter Series 2) are Red/Green and Yellow Digivice cards.

The game mats included with both games also hint at a change in the gameplay for the English version (mainly due to fewer spaces for cards to be played). ➔

Four-card boosters (left) are sold in Japanse vending machines, while U.S. boosters (above) contain eight cards and come in traditional Mylar packs.

Digimon 29

Digimon Special Feature
Game Overview

Digimon versus Pokémon

The major differences from the Pokémon CCG are:
- Deck size in Digimon is 30 cards (as opposed to 60).
- No duplicates are allowed (i.e., only one ST-1 Agumon is allowed in the deck). Additional Agumon will be available in subsequent boosters, so you'll have the opportunity to have another Agumon with a different card number in your deck.
- You cannot lose by "decking" (running out of cards). Once your Online stack (draw pile) is empty, you discard your hand and remove all cards except your current Rookie from your side of the board and put them in your Offline stack (discard pile/ graveyard). Then you shuffle your Offline stack and make it your new Online stack.
- There are no Energy cards (as in Pokémon) to be attached, nor is there any need for Land or Mana cards (as in Magic: The Gathering). There are also no cards that allow deck manipulation, card searching or card drawing.
- Hand size is 10 cards (six cards in Japan). At the end of the Attack phase, you refresh your hand size to 10 cards.
- Some Digimon have "comes-into-play" effects that occur when the creature enters the game. Other Digimon have special effects that occur when they win, lose or tie.

You earn victory points based on the level of the Digimon you defeat.
- The losing Digimon devolves to the Rookie level after the battle is over.

Unlike Pokémon and Magic, Digimon has no Energy or Land cards for powering-up attacks or summoning monsters.

Evolutionary Trees

Despite the differences from more familiar CCGs like Pokémon and Magic, the Digi-Battle game seems to require an equal amount of strategy. Just to show how many cards have to fall just right, let's start with the Mega Digimon Saber Leomon (one of the biggest evolutions in the game) and trace its evolutionary tree backwards. To get a Saber Leomon, you must have previously combined Piximon with Triceramon (one of these is your Duel Zone Digimon, the other is a Champion card in your hand).

To get to Piximon, you would've had to combine Tortamon with Gekomon, Monochromon with Starmon or Dokugumon with Rockmon (again, for all three cases, one card is in the Duel Zone and the other in your hand).

Digimon are differentiated into four Digivolve levels: Rookie, Champion, Ultimate and Mega.

The Triceramon path is a little easier because you only need to have Starmon, Monochromon or Greymon and the appropriate Digivice. To get to Tortamon, you must start with Tentomon, Otamamon or Gotsumon. The same for Gekomon. Going the Monochromon route is not possible with the starter set because the Rookie that it Digivolves from is not in the Starter series (but it is in the Booster series).

Starmon sprouts from Otamamon or Gotsumon. Dokugumon results from Biyomon or Palmon. To get to Rockmon, you need to start as Biyomon or Agumon. And lastly, everyone should know that Agumon leads to Greymon. You clear on that?

So there you have it: 16 cards in this family tree (and at least one to three more to get to Monochromon). Since the deck size is 30 cards, I could easily use the remaining space in the deck for Power Option cards — Force FX, Digivolve and Power Blast. There just doesn't appear to be room for a second family tree to another Mega Digimon that might share common Rookies, Champions or Ultimates with the primary tree — unless you play fast and loose with the necessary Power Option cards you need to get to your Mega Digimon. ➜

Digimon Special Feature
Game Overview

U.S. Series-1 Boosters

With only three potential Mega family trees present in the Starter, the environment could grow quite stale in a hurry. Luckily, Upper Deck followed the debut release with a 54-card booster series in March and April.

In early March, I found booster packs at my local Toys "R" Us. These cards fill in some of the creatures that were alluded to in the starter (such as Tapirmon and Monochromon). The set also features three more rainbow-foil cards (Metal Seadramon, Metal Etemon and one other) plus three gold-embossed cards (Boltmon, Marine Angemon and Gatomon). New Power Option cards give your Digimon special powers like fly, dig or swim, and other cards reduce the attacks of Digimon with specific special powers.

Overall, the addition of the Series-1 boosters makes the game a lot more fun to play and should greatly increase its longevity.

Series-1 boosters contain many cards alluded to in the starter set.

32 Digimon

Digimon Rules (Literally)

All you need to play a game

A. SETUP

1. Spread out all 62 Digi-Battle cards face-up on a flat surface. Flip a coin to decide who goes first. Players take turns choosing cards, one at a time, until each has created a Battle Deck of 30 cards. Put the two leftover cards aside. (Players may agree to play with their own previously customized Battle Decks. These can include any 30 different cards. No duplicates.)
2. Each selects a Rookie card from the deck and places it face down on the Duel Zone.
3. Each shuffles the remaining 29 cards, deals himself or herself 10 and places the remaining 19 cards face down online.
4. Each turns over the Rookie card in the Duel Zone.

Players now see which card their opponent has played and note its battle type: red, green or yellow. They then refer to the chart on their card showing the amount of Digimon Power they can blast at that type of opponent. The player who displays the higher amount of Digimon Power has the advantage, and, if no more cards are played, wins the Duel.

The players now review the 10 cards in their hand and consider strategy. To increase the amount of Digimon Power you can blast at your opponent, you'll probably want to Digivolve to the next level. Proceed to the Digivolve phase.

(Tip: When choosing your Battle Deck, make sure to include an evolutionary "tree" of Digimon that can Digivolve to the highest levels. One way to do this is to build backward from the Mega level, making sure to pick Digimon that appear in the Digivolve Requirements of the cards you've chosen in descending order. To find "family trees," notice the backgrounds behind the Digimon.)

(Tip: Make sure to include enough Power Option cards to give yourself Power Options.)

B. DIGIVOLVE

Both players review their hands, and if they have a card that Digivolves their Digimon to the next level, they place it face-down on the Digivolve Zone. This new next-level card must show the name of the Digimon currently on the Duel Zone in its Digivolve Requirements box, and you must be prepared to fulfill any other Digivolve Requirements stated there.

To determine if two Digimon are from the same "evolutionary tree," compare their backgrounds

1. Flip a coin to decide who goes first.
2. Player who goes first turns over the card on the Digivolve Zone and places it face up on top of the card on the Duel Zone.
3. Player completes turn by fulfilling any Digivolve Requirements shown on the next-level card. For example: →

Digimon Special Feature
Game Overview

Digivolving from Rookie to Champion requires moving one or two cards from Online to Offline as "payment." (See example below.) Digivolving from Champion to Ultimate or from Ultimate to Mega requires that you either:

a) Place a Digivice Power Option* card on the Power Port, or

b) DNA Digivolve, which means you must play two lower-level cards instead of one. You do this by placing the second Digimon (the one not showing on the Duel Zone) face-up on the Power Port when you turn over the next-level Digimon on the Duel Zone.

*Note: There are two other Power Option cards that can be used in the Digivolve Phase: Ultra Digivolve and Digivolve To Champion. See instructions in the Effects section of each card for use.

After the first player has finished Digivolving, the second player notes any changes in Digimon Power and may respond by either Digivolving as shown above, or deciding not to Digivolve and saying "Pass." If the player who passes has a card face down on the Digivolve Zone, he must move it Offline; in other words, "use it or lose it." If a player doesn't have a card to Digivolve, he or she must pass. If both players do not have cards in hand to Digivolve, proceed to the Battle phase.

You may Digivolve only one level per Duel. After each player has either Digivolved or passed, the Digivolve phase is over. Proceed to the Battle phase.

C. BATTLE

Starting with the winner of the coin toss, players now take turns playing Power Option cards on the Power Port, one card per turn. Each Power Option card has an Effect that you can use to try for an advantage over your opponent. Some Power Option cards have Use Requirements attached to their Effect. You must complete these Use Requirements as part of your turn for the Effect to come into play. Keep track of how the dueling Digimon's relative strength changes with each card played, as shown by comparing Digimon Power.

Continue taking turns until a player runs out of Power Option cards to play, or decides to stop playing them and says "Pass." The other player may continue to play Power Option cards until he or she runs out of cards or decides to stop.

When the play stops, the player displaying the most Digimon Power wins the Duel.

The winner scores points depending on the Digivolve Level (Rookie, Champion, Ultimate, Mega) of the defeated opponent, as shown in the Score section at the bottom of the winning card. Winner adds the new points to his score counter.

The winner keeps all Digimon on the Duel zone. Defeated player sends all Digimon except the Rookie Offline. Both players send all Power Option cards Offline.

The winner goes first in the next Duel.

In the event of a tie, all Digimon remain on the Duel Zone and all Power Option cards are sent Offline. No points are scored. Winner of the previous Duel (or of the coin toss) goes first in the next Duel.

The first player to score 1,000 points wins the game.

The winner of each Digibattle scores points based on the Digivolve level (Rookie, Champion, etc.) of the defeated Digimon

D. REGROUP

First, restore your hand to 10 cards by drawing from the Online deck. Players may discard as many cards from their remaining hand to Offline as they wish, and draw as many new cards from the Online deck as needed to restore their hand to 10 cards. This is the only time when you may restore your hand.

When there are not enough cards remaining in the Online deck to restore your hand to 10 cards, draw down to zero, then send all the cards on your side of the board Offline except the Rookie. Shuffle them and place them face-down Online. You may then draw as many as needed to restore your hand to 10 cards.

Note: If at any time during play the number of your Online cards goes down to zero (either by your action or your opponent's), you must send all the cards on your side of the board Offline except the Rookie, then shuffle them and place them face down Online before resuming play.

At this point, players have the option of changing their Rookie (if they have one on the Duel Zone). To set up a change, place the new Rookie face down on top of the old Rookie. If you have a card with the Requirements to Digivolve your new Rookie to the next level, you would use it now by placing it face down on the Digivolve Zone. (Both cards will be turned over when it's your turn to Digivolve.)

Players may prepare to Digivolve any Digimon on their Duel Zone by placing the next-level card (with the correct Digivolve Requirements) face down on the Digivolve Zone.

The winner of the last Duel initiates the new Duel by starting at step No. 2 of the Digivolve process. If the last Duel ended in a tie, the player who went first last time initiates the new Duel.

(Tip: Take time to become familiar with your Digimon. They each have a unique personality. Many of them have special abilities, and some of them have powerful special effects that you can use to your advantage in Digimon Digi-Battle!)

DIGIMON DIGI-BATTLE FACTS

What are Digimon?
Digimon are Digital Monsters that live on File Island. You can match them in battles with one another to see who has more power. With your help, they can Digivolve into more powerful monsters to increase their chances of winning.

How many can play?
Two.

What do you need to play?
Two Battle Decks of 30 different Digi-Battle cards each — a total of 60 cards (62 provided with Starter Set 1), one game mat and two score counters.

What is the basic premise of the game?
Players face each other across the game mat. They each select Digimon cards from their Battle Decks to do battle in the Duel Zone. Digimon Power data on the cards will show, depending on the Battle Type of the opponent, who has more relative strength. As the Digimon Digivolve to more powerful forms in the Digivolve Phase, and as they acquire different powers and identities with the help of Power Option cards in the Battle Phase, their relative strength will change. When both players have finished playing their Power Option cards, the Battle Phase is complete, and Digimon Power data on the cards will show who has won the Duel. The winner of the Duel is awarded points.

How do you score points?
The winner scores points as shown in the Score section at the bottom of the winning Digimon card, based on the Digivolve Level (Rookie, Champion, Ultimate, Mega) of the defeated opponent.

How do you win the game?
The first to score 1,000 points wins the game.

Can I customize my Battle Deck?
Yes! Players may agree to play with Battle Decks they've put together before the game. These customized Battle Decks can be composed of any 30 different cards. ➜

Digimon Special Feature
Game Overview

DIGIMON DIGI-BATTLE CARDS

There are two kinds of cards: Digimon cards and Power Option cards. Digimon cards are the character cards that fight their battles in the Duel Zone. Power Option cards are used to enhance the power and flexibility of the battling Digimon cards.

The cards are available in one complete Starter Set. The Starter Set contains 62 different cards, a game mat, 2 score counters, and an instruction sheet. There are 48 different Digimon cards and 14 different Power Option cards. The cards in the Starter Set are identified by an "ST-" prefix to their card number.

DIGIMON CARDS

Digimon cards are divided into three Battle Types: red, green and yellow. The Battle Type of your opponent is what determines your relative Digimon Power. This relationship changes from card to card, as shown in the Digimon Power chart on each Digimon card. In general, yellow is more powerful than green, and green is more powerful than red, but at times red is more powerful than yellow. You can think of this as similar to the relationships in "Rock, Scissors, Paper."

They are further differentiated into four Digivolve levels. These levels are, in ascending order: Rookie, Champion, Ultimate, and Mega. The higher the level, the stronger the card. To Digivolve your battling Digimon to the next level, you must play a card that meets the Digivolve requirements. The Digivolve Requirements are shown in a box at the top of the card.

POWER OPTION CARDS

Power Option cards come in three types: Digivolve, Force FX and Power Blast cards.

Digivolve cards are used in the Digivolve Phase to evolve the battling Digimon to a more powerful state. Be sure to read the effects described on the Digivolve cards.

Force FX cards are used in the Battle Phase to change the color of your Digimon Power — red, green or yellow — regardless of the Battle Type of your opponent.

Power Blast cards are used in the Battle Phase to enhance the battling Digimon in several different ways, depending on what is printed on the card. Be sure to read the effects described on the Power Blast cards. Digimon

(Above) Digimon Battle Types (red, yellow and green) share a sort of "rock, scissors, paper" relationship of relative strength

DIGI-BATTLE STARTER-SET CARD LIST

ROOKIE DIGIMON (12)

ST-01 Agumon
ST-03 Biyomon
ST-05 Gabumon
ST-07 Tentomon
ST-09 Palmon
ST-11 Gomamon
ST-13 Patamon
ST-18 Kunemon
ST-23 Gotsumon
ST-24 Otamamon
ST-41 Candlemon
ST-42 DemiDevimon

CHAMPION DIGIMON (22)

ST-02 Greymon
ST-04 Birdramon
ST-06 Garurumon
ST-08 Kabuterimon
ST-10 Togemon
ST-12 Ikkakumon
ST-14 Angemon
ST-15 Nanimon
ST-16 Unimon
ST-17 Centarumon
ST-19 Dokugumon
ST-20 Musyamon
ST-22 Rockmon
ST-25 Tortomon
ST-26 Starmon
ST-27 Gekomon
ST-35 Dolphmon
ST-36 Coelamon
ST-37 Octomon
ST-43 Apemon
ST-44 Wizardmon
ST-45 Bakemon

ULTIMATE DIGIMON (11)

ST-21 Kimeramon
ST-28 MegaKabuterimon
ST-29 Triceramon
ST-30 Piximon
ST-31 Okuwamon
ST-32 SkullGreymon
ST-38 Zudomon
ST-39 MarineDevimon
ST-46 Mammothmon
ST-47 WereGarurumon
ST-48 SkullMeramon

MEGA DIGIMON (3)

ST-33 HerculesKabuterimon
ST-34 SaberLeomon
ST-40 Pukumon

FORCE FX (3)

ST-49 Red Offensive
ST-50 Yellow Offensive
ST-51 Green Offensive

DIGIVOLVE (6)

ST-55 Digivolve to Champion
ST-56 Ultra Digivolve
ST-59 Digivice Red
ST-60 Digivice Green & Yellow
ST-61 Digivice Red & Green
ST-62 Digivice Yellow

POWER BLAST (5)

ST-52 Blitz
ST-53 Metal Attack
ST-54 Counter Attack!
ST-57 Downgrade
ST-58 Digi-Duel

Check out www.bandai.com (from which the preceding has been derived) for more information, examples, tips, and details.

There are three types of Power Option cards: Digivolve, Force and Power Blast.

Pet The

Digimon

The original Digimon toys still pack a wallop

By Gordon Kane

HERE'S A QUESTION: WHEN DID YOU become aware of Digimon?

For some, the ride started with the August 1999 debut of the animated series. Others learned of Digimon through the virtual-pet games found in toy stores in early 1998.

I became aware of Digimon around July 1997, thanks to an online acquaintance, during the excitement generated by the American release of Tamagotchi. People on that now-defunct e-mail list were embroiled in a hot debate over whether Tamagotchi was just for girls. (I can't remember how the debate went, but the sides were pretty well dug in.)

In the midst of the fray, one of the more-informed debaters mentioned a similar device called Digimon that was supposedly targeted at boys. In addition to raising an electronic creature, Digimon allowed you to engage monsters in other Digimon devices in pixelated battles. Evolution was based on the care provided and success in battle.

I had to have one. After much searching and pleading, I was able to buy a pair of Japanese Digimon (because a single one couldn't realize its fully evolved potential — oh, those marketing geniuses at Bandai), and my addiction to Digimon began.

In Japan, Bandai released Digimon in two color variations — a blue/gray shell and a red/brown shell — and expanded the color palette to include red, dark green, blue and yellow a few months later. The color variations →

Pet The Digimon

were intoxicating to a collector like myself, and while I couldn't afford to have them all, knowledge of the variations was sufficient for the time being.

Once I pulled the tab and set the time, I was introduced to the Fresh Digimon Botamon, the In-Training Digimon Koromon and two Rookie Digimon, Agumon and Betamon. I had to wait a couple of days before I met any Champion Digimon: Greymon, Tyrannomon, Meramon, Airdramon, Seadramon, Devimon and Numemon. And I had to wait a few more days for a glimpse of an Ultimate Digimon: Metal Greymon, Mamemon and Monzaemon.

When one monster died I started over, striving to get a monster I hadn't had before. For the most part I met with success, but I drove a few family members and co-workers crazy in the process. (Turning the sound off doesn't win you any friends, but it goes a long way against making new enemies.)

Six months later, Bandai released Digimon in North America in four color variations — blue/gray, red/brown, bright yellow and dark blue. Devimon and Monzaemon received name changes and were now known as Darkmon and Teddymon. Luckily, the Japanese and English devices had no trouble negotiating the language barrier because my Japanese Digimon and my English Digimon happily battled each other.

During this time, an online community of Digimon trainers and tamers sprang up. We exchanged all sorts of information on the monsters and what sort of care, feeding, training and battle regimens were required to get specific Champions or the desired Ultimate.

Digivolving was never a problem for me; almost every time I got a Greymon, it became a Metal Greymon. Every Betamon became a Meramon and almost every Meramon became a Mamemon.

I had to wait several months, however, before I got a Numemon to become a Teddymon. Many found it strange that the most sickly character (Numemon) could become the most desirable character (Teddymon), but Japanese lore is full of utter failures who rise above their situation to become the hero. My biggest problem was getting all the Champions; to this day, I have yet to raise a Tyrannomon, Airdramon or Seadramon.

While American youth was enjoying its Digimon, Bandai released Digimon 2 and Digimon 3 in Japan. We figured Bandai America would follow suit. The company even posted a sales sheet on its Web site stating that action figures and Digimon 2 would be coming in spring 1998. We waited patiently, but they never appeared. We did see additional color variations of Digimon 1: transparent red, transparent blue, transparent yellow and transparent lime green in February 1998 followed by green, red, smoke and clear in December 1998.

Bandai Japan kept churning out Digimon, continuing with Digimon 4 and Digimon 5. Each game was an improvement over its predecessors, but the degree of advancement was slight. Some of these games are little more than variations of previous units that featured different monsters. ➜

In addition to nurturing an electronic feature, Digimon allows you to engage monsters in other Digimon devices in pixelated battles. Evolution is based on care provided and success in battle.

The color variations can be interesting fodder for Digimon collectors, with their unique tones and shades.

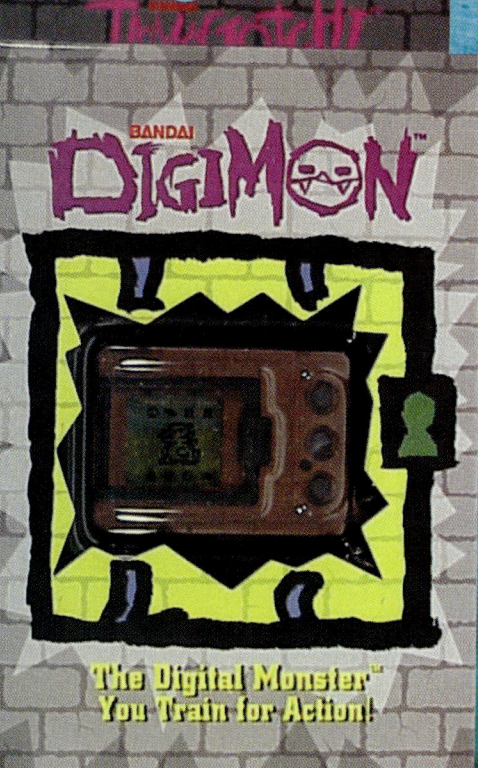

Digimon 41

Pet The Digimon

All that changed, and real improvements occurred after Bandai changed the toy's shape, added more monsters and increased functionality. These new Digimon hand-held games were called Digimon Pendulum.

The Pendulums were a genuine step forward. Like the first Digimon games, they were also released in multiple versions, the latest being Pendulum 5. They were very successful in Japan and continued to push forward the product side of Digimon through 1999.

Pendulum 5 was brought to market concurrently with the Digivice, the newest generation of Bandai electronic pets. Bandai changed the shape of the unit again, and it does more than any previous Digimon pet.

The device is made to look like a piece of technology all the kids possess in the animation series, and you get to choose one of the Digi-Destined's Rookies (Agumon, Gabumon, Palmon, Patamon, Gomamon, Biyomon or Tentomon) for your starting Digimon.

My Japanese Digivice is bigger than the Digimon or Digimon Pendulum, and costs more, too ($19-21 versus $28). Nothing is in English, so you have to start it up and fumble your way around until you figure out which buttons control which function.

All seven of the Rookie Digimon are in the device, which operates on a walk-around basis — that is, it counts the steps you take and makes them steps in the Digimon adventure. After so many steps, you fight.

The shortcut is to shake the Digivice until you get to a fight, but this technique has pluses and minuses. If you shake it and then neglect it for a while, it'll fight without you, and your Digimon will get trounced.

If your Digimon do get trounced, you have to find the medical kit to heal them. If you want to fight hard, keep pressing the button in the upper right-hand corner. Eventually you'll figure out how to get your Digimon vitamins and Power Ups so they can evolve.

Everything is actually pretty simple; the only screen that might be confusing is the battle screen. When you are in your first 10 matches, there are only two options: Use Current Digimon or Quick Fight. You should select "Use Current Digimon" and keep pressing until a weapon is launched. After three attacks, or when someone's Hit Points go down to zero, the battle is over. You lose if a skull appears.

If you select "Quick Fight," the fight happens without any animation and then the results are announced. (I have lost all but one Quick Fight; my advice is to avoid them.)

After 10 victories, your battle screen offers three options: Use Current Digimon, Digivolve or Quick Fight. This is slightly misleading because you can't actually use the Digivolve function until you win 15 more battles. With 25 total wins under your belt you can Digivolve on your second turn of a fight.

After you rescue one of the other seven Digimon and they join your adventure party, your battle screen will feature these options: Use Current Digimon, Digivolve, Switch Digimon and Quick Fight. What's neat about these encounters is that there's a different screen and a flashing LED to signal that one of the good Digimon needs your help.

So far, Palmon and Gabumon have joined my quest, and Agumon is able to Digivolve to Greymon and Metal Greymon. I'm campaigning Palmon as my primary creature so that I can Digivolve to her higher versions. I've encountered many Gazimon and Sukamon and have seen quite a few Bakemon. I've also come across Kawagamon, and I suspect I'll see Etemon and Myotismon in the future. ➜

These hand-held toys nicely round out Bandai's family of virtual pets.

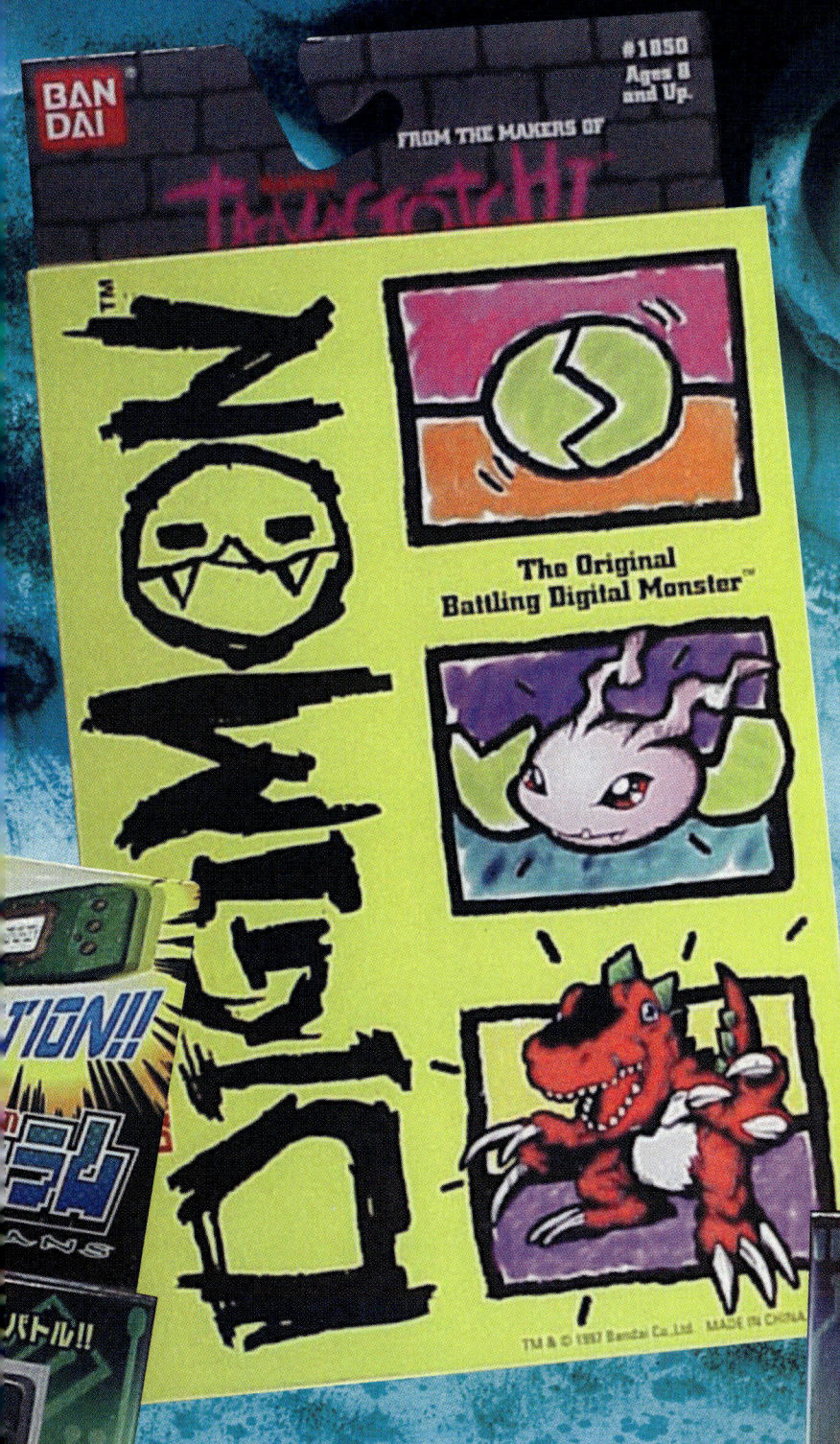

Everything is actually pretty simple; the only screen that might be confusing is the battle screen.

Digimon 43

Pet The Digimon

The device looks like a piece of technology all the kids possess in the animation series.

Overall, my Digivice is pretty cool. It's a nice addition to the family of Bandai v-pets. It'll drive the school folk crazy, though, because it's not as unobtrusive as Pocket Pikachu — mainly because you need to hear when you encounter a bad guy. If you turn off the sound and miss the bad guy, your Digimon will take damage anyway.

Bandai America has announced that the Digivice should be in the retail outlets by the end of April. Let's hope so. Meanwhile, in Japan there's already a Digivice 2 available for purchase in the toy stores.

There's always been a demand for the Digimon hand-helds that never were available in America, but inquiries regarding their availability have exploded. The animated series has raised awareness of the number of products that existed before the series premiered. Along with increased awareness have come higher prices.

Sadly, only Pendulum 3, 4 and 5 seem to be readily available, and these three only partially represent the Digi-Destined's Digimon. Occasionally, other models pop up on auction sites, but the final price is often beyond the spending power of the average Digimon fanatic. Hopefully, the Digivice will adequately substitute for previously produced and hard-to-find Digimon devices.

An English-language Digivice would seem to be the perfect introduction to the multitudes whose answer to the question, "When did you become aware of Digimon?" would be "a month ago," "two weeks ago" or even "yesterday." They're out there — and the Digivice will be their toy. And if not, rest assured that Bandai will have a new generation of toys just for them. *Digimon*

Virtually Impossible

A guide to the hard-to-find Japanese Digimon v-pets

As mentioned in the main article, Bandai Japan has released many more Digimon virtual-pet games in Japan (and elsewhere) than in North America.

Following the success of Digimon 1 in Japan, Bandai released Digimon 2 in September 1997. This version included 14 new monsters:
Fresh: Punimon
In-Training: Tsunomom
Rookies: Gabumon and Elecmon
Champions: Garurumon, Birdramon, Kabuterimon, Whamon, Angemon, Frigimon, VegieMon
Ultimates: Metal Mamemon, Skull Greymon and Vademon

The package can be identified by the picture of Garurumon. The devices initially came in black and white, with transparent-smoke and transparent-colorless variations arriving later.

Bandai released Digimon 3 in December 1997. This version included 14 new monsters:
Fresh: Poyomon
In-Training: Tokumon
Rookies: Kunemon and Patamon
Champions: Unimon, Centaurmon, Ogremon, Bakemon, Shellmon, Drimogemon and Sukamon
Ultimates: Etemon, Giromon and Andromon

The package can be identified by the picture of Ogremon. The devices initially came in orange and purple, with transparent-orange and transparent-purple variations arriving later.

Bandai released Digimon 4 in March 1998. This version included 14 new monsters:
Fresh: Yuramon
In-Training: Tanemon
Rookies: Piyomon and Palmon
Champions: Monokuromon, Kokitorimon, Leomon, Kuwagamon, Seelamon, Mojamon and Nanimon
Ultimates: Digitamamon, Piximon and MegaDramon

The package can be identified by the picture of Kuwagamon, and the devices came in two colors — transparent red and transparent blue.

Bandai released Digimon 5 in June 1998. This version included 14 new monsters:
Fresh: Zurumon
In-Training: Pugmon
Rookies: Gizamon and Gajimon
Champions: Dark Tyrannomon, Cyclomon, Devidramon, Tuskmon, Flymon, Deltamon and Raremon
Ultimates: Metal Tyrannomon, Datamon, ExTyrannomon

This is the rarest of the Digimon, with a very short production run, as Bandai was gearing up for the launch of the Digimon Pendulum. The package can be identified by the picture of two connected devices, and the device came only in transparent green.

In September 1998, Bandai Japan changed the look of the Digimon game/toy and added an additional level in the creature hierarchy: Mega. Bandai added a mechanic to the device, the pendulum, that was used to determine the monster's strength during a given training session or battle. A specific number of shakes ensured peak performance, and once that number was discovered, it could be duplicated in subsequent training sessions and battle scenarios as long as that creature existed. There was also an additional mechanic called JOGRES, which allowed two Digimon tamers to combine their creatures to create new yet predictable monsters. One other interesting note: Bandai incorporated 100-percent-English menus into the Pendulums, unlike the prior models.

The first Pendulum model, Nature Spirits, featured 20 monsters:
Fresh: Babumon
In-Training: Motimon
Rookies: Tentomon, Gotsumon, and Otamamon
Champions: Kabuterimon, Tortamon, Monochromon, Starmon, Kuwagamon and Gekomon
Ultimates: MegaKabuterimon, Jyagamon, Triceramon, Piximon, Okuwamon and Shogun Gekomon
Megas: Hercules Kabuterimon, Saber Leomon and Metal Etemon

The package can be identified by the picture of Triceramon, and the device came in silver (some with blue buttons, others with black buttons).

After three attacks, or when someone's Hit Points go down to zero, the battle is over.

In December 1998, the Pendulum series continued with the second Pendulum model, Deep Savers. It featured 20 monsters:
Fresh: Pitchmon
In-Training: Pukamon
Rookies: Gomamon, Crabmon and Syakomon
Champions: Ikkakumon, Zukamon, Seadramon, Coelamon, Dolphmon and Octmon
Ultimates: Zudomon, Whamon, MegaSeadramon, Scorpiomon, Marine Devimon and Dragomon
Megas: Marine Angemon, Metal Seadramon and Pukamon

The package has a picture of Dolphmon, and the device came in blue (some with orange buttons, others with black buttons).

In March 1999, the Pendulum series continued with the release of the third Pendulum model, Nightmare Soldiers. It featured 20 monsters:
Fresh: Mokumon
In-Training: Petite Meramon
Rookies: Bakumon, Candmon and Demidevimon
Champions: Apemon, Garurumon, Meramon, Wizardmon, Devimon and Bakemon
Ultimates: Mammothmon, WereGarurumon, Skull Meramon, Pumpkinmon, Myotismon and Phantomon
Megas: Skull Mammothmon, Boltmon, Piedmon

The package has a picture of Wizardmon, and the device came in red (some with blue buttons, others with black buttons).

In June 1999, the series continued with the fourth Pendulum model, Wind Guardians:
Fresh: Nyokimon
In-Training: Pyocomon
Rookies: Piyomon, Floramon and Mushroomon
Champions: Veedramon, Birdramon, Togemon, Kiwimon, Woodmon and Red Vegiemon

Ultimates: Aero Veedramon, Garudamon, Blossomon, Delumon, Cherrymon and Garbagemon
Megas: Phoenixmon, Gryphonmon and Puppetmon

The package has a picture of Veedramon, and the device came in green (some with yellow buttons, others with black buttons).

In July 1999, Bandai released two toys that weren't quite Digimon virtual pets but acted like them. The toy Talking Agumon and Talking Patamon allowed you to use the talking toy to fight your virtual pet — but instead of seeing the talking pet fight, you heard it fight.

In September 1999, the Pendulum series continued with the release of the fifth Pendulum model, Metal Empire. It featured 20 monsters:
Fresh: Choromon
In-Training: Kapurimon
Rookies: Toy Agumon, Kokuwamon and Hagurumon
Champions: Greymon, Rebelmon, Tankmon, Clockmon, Guardmon and Mecha Norimon
Ultimates: Metal Greymon, Andromon, Knightmon, MegaMamemon, Metal Dramon and WereMonzaemon
Megas: WereGreymon, Metal Garurumon, Machine Dramon

The package can be identified by the picture of Metal Greymon, and the device came in black (some with blue buttons, others with red buttons).

At the same time the Metal Empire Pendulum was released, Bandai introduced a device that closely resembled the piece of technology carried by the kids on the animated series. The Digivice allowed you to start with one of the seven Digidestined's Digimon (Kari had not been added to the group).

As your quest progresses, you gain the ability to Digivolve to the Ultimate. The bad Digimon you encounter along the way are primarily the ones introduced in the Devimon and Etemon story lines. These came in transparent orange (with Greymon on the box) and transparent blue (with Garurumon on the box).

In December 1999, Digivice 2 arrived in Japan. Once again, you can start as one of the seven — which is curious, because the transparent pink Digivice has Gatomon on the box, so you might think that you'd begin the quest as Gatomon. The other Digivice is a transparent light blue with Agumon on the box. I don't know if this Digivice will allow me to Warp Digivolve to WereGreymon. However, the evil Digimon appear to be the villains of the Myotismon story lines and might extend to include the Dark Masters storyline.

In addition to all these toys, there's one Digimon virtual pet I haven't mentioned: the Digimon Adventure game for WonderSwan (Bandai's attempt to enter the hand-held marketplace, similar to the GameBoy or Sega GameGear). The WonderSwan game allows you to raise multiple Digimon from the five Japanese Digimon virtual-pet devices. On the WonderSwan you raise, feed and train monsters like the virtual-pet devices, and you can even battle Digimon, Pendulum, Digivice and Talking toys through an attachment that comes with the Digimon Adventure game cartridge. The game also allows you to assemble a team of the Digimon you are raising and campaign them against a team of computer Digimon. *Digimon*

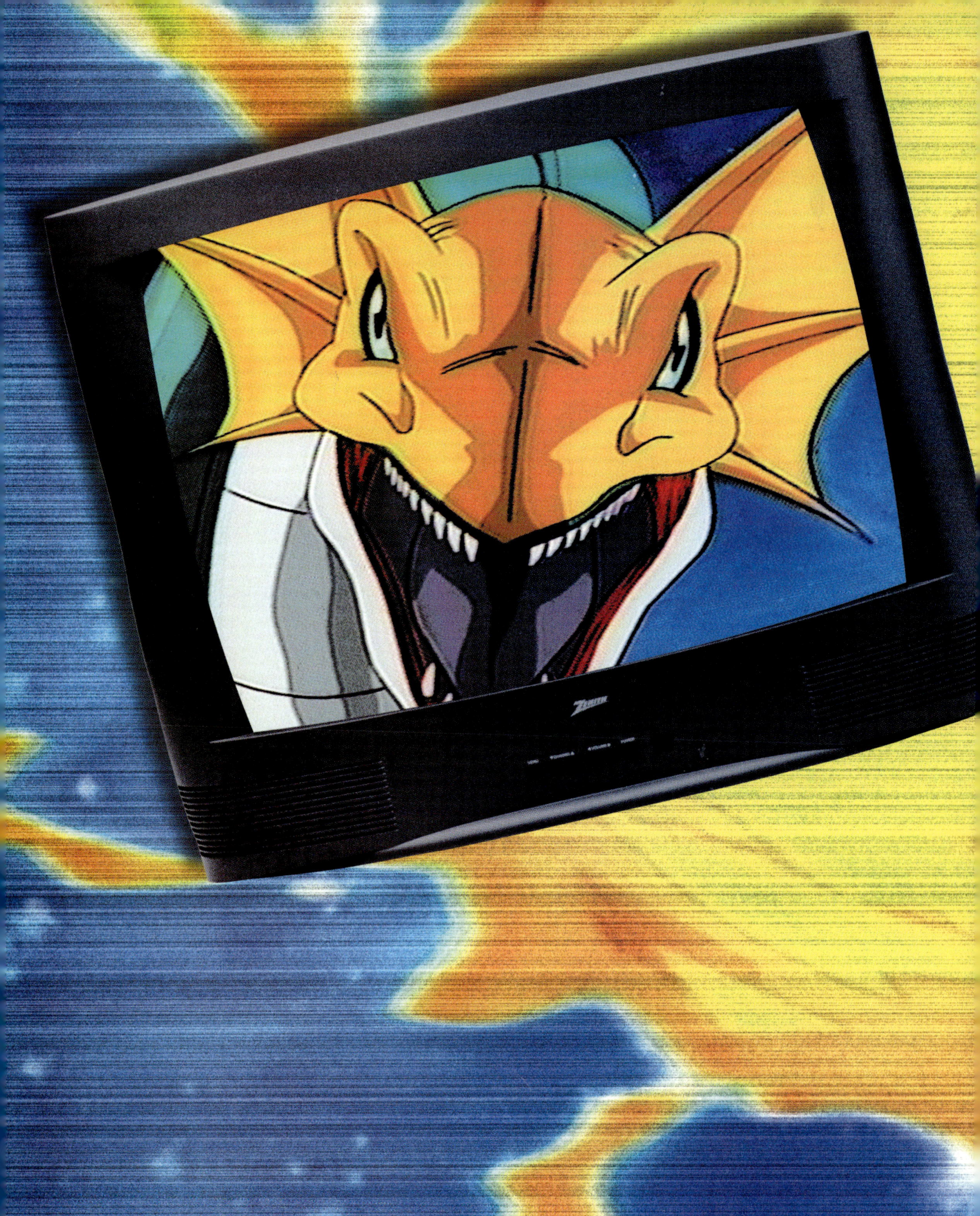

Daring Digital Adventures

A guided tour through *Digimon Adventures'* 54 breathtaking episodes

By Grace Anderson

ALTHOUGH DIGIMON may have started out as a hand-held game, the animated TV series *Digimon Adventures* has really propelled Digimon to popularity in North America and Japan. Fifty-two of the 54 episodes made have been shown so far in Japan, while 42 have aired in North America.

A second season of episodes began April 2 in Japan, and while Saban has picked it up for North American release, there's no set date for its premiere.

With its high-quality animation and great blend of comedy and adventure, *Digimon Adventures* has become a favorite with kids, teens and adults. →

At first, the kids don't know what to make of these strange new monsters, the Digimon.

Episode 1: And So It Begins

The first episode introduces the seven DigiDestined (known as the Chosen Children in Japan) and their Digimon partners. Tai, Matt, Sora, Izzy, Joe, Mimi and T.K. are at summer camp when they get transported to the Digiworld. There they meet Koromon, Tsunomon, Yokomon, Motimon, Bukamon, Tanemon and Tokomon, their partner Digimon. They also have their first run-in with an enemy Digimon, Kuwagamon, and their partners Digivolve to defeat the enemy.

Although many small changes were made from the original Japanese version, the biggest change in this episode is that the North American version neglects to mention how old the children are. Joe is in sixth grade, Tai, Matt and Sora are in fifth, Mimi and Izzy are in fourth, and T.K. is in second.

Episode 2: The Birth of Greymon

After their battle with Kuwagamon, the children find themselves on a beach with their newly Digivolved Digimon: Agumon, Gabumon, Biyomon, Tentomon, Gomamon, Palmon and Patamon. Everything seems safe until they're attacked once again, this time by an even stronger enemy, Shellmon. Their Digimon are no match for Shellmon, so Tai's partner, Agumon, Digivolves once more into Greymon and saves the day.

Episode 3: Garurumon the Blue Wolf

The children find a train by the side of a lake and, tired from walking around the island, decide to sleep there for the night. There's only one problem: The train is sitting on Seadramon's back. Matt is caught by Seadramon when he tries to help out his little brother T.K., and Gabumon Digivolves into Garurumon to rescue Matt.

In the North American version, Matt tells the other children that T.K. is his half-brother. In the original, they were full brothers.

Episode 4: Biyomon Gets Firepower

Emerging from the forest onto a savanna, the children arrive at a Yokomon village. Mount Miharashi, the source of the village's water, was guarded by Meramon, but an accident occurred and the water dried up. To save Sora and the village from Meramon's attack, Biyomon evolves into Birdramon and defeats Meramon. The children discover that Meramon was being controlled by a Black Gear that had fallen from the sky.

Episode 5: Kabuterimon's Electro Shocker

At a factory outside of the savanna the children come across Andromon, who was caught in a machine and unable to move. Even though Andromon is supposedly a good Digimon, he attacks the children. Izzy uses his computer to make Tentomon evolve into Kabuterimon and defeat Andromon. It turns out that Andromon was being controlled by a Black Gear.

Episode 6: Togemon in Toy Town

The children are attacked by a group of Numemon in an underground passage. Mimi and Palmon run away but are then attacked by Monzaemon and get lost in Toy Town. Monzaemon captures the other children, who have their emotions erased. Palmon Digivolves into Togemon and defeats Monzaemon, who was also being controlled by a Black Gear.

Episode 7: Ikkakumon's Harpoon Torpedo

Unable to proceed any further, the children begin to fight among themselves. As the oldest, Joe feels it's his duty to stop the fighting, so he decides to climb the mountain and find the source of the Black Gears. There he meets Unimon, another Digimon possessed by a Black Gear. The other children come looking for Joe and are also attacked by Unimon. Gomamon saves the day by Digivolving into Ikkakumon. The children reach the top of Infinity Mountain and find that File Island is just a small island in the middle of a huge ocean.

Episode 8: Evil Shows His Face

The children rest in a house they find, but it turns out to be a trap set by Devimon. Leomon, a good Digimon controlled by a Black Gear, and an evil Digimon, Ogremon, attack the children. The Digimon Digivolve and try to attack Devimon, but he is too strong for them. The island begins to break up and the children are separated from each other.

There was a scene cut from the North American version of this episode. Originally when the children were taking a bath, there was a shot from behind of Joe, Matt and Tai naked.

Episode 9: Sub-zero Ice Punch

Tai and Agumon end up in a frozen wasteland. There they are attacked by Frigimon, who was being controlled by a Black Gear. Once they remove his Black Gear, Frigimon helps them find Matt and Gabumon, who have landed nearby. Matt and Tai fight about what to do next, but eventually decide to return to Infinity Mountain.

Episode 10: A Clue from the Digi-Past

Mimi and Palmon meet up with Izzy and Tentomon in the Dino Ruins. Mimi tries to get Izzy to help her find the others, but he's so enthralled with the ruins that he doesn't want to leave. They are attacked by a Black Gear Digimon, Centaurmon. Once he is returned to normal he tells them about their Digivices.

Episode 11: The Dancing Digimon

Joe and Gomamon meet up with Sora and Biyomon. They are captured by a group of Bakemon and are about to be sacrificed. With help from Joe, Ikkakumon and Birdramon defeat the Bakemon and escape.

In the Japanese version, Joe chanted Buddhist sutras to weaken the Bakemon. ➜

The DigiDestined and their Digimon partners quickly become the best of friends.

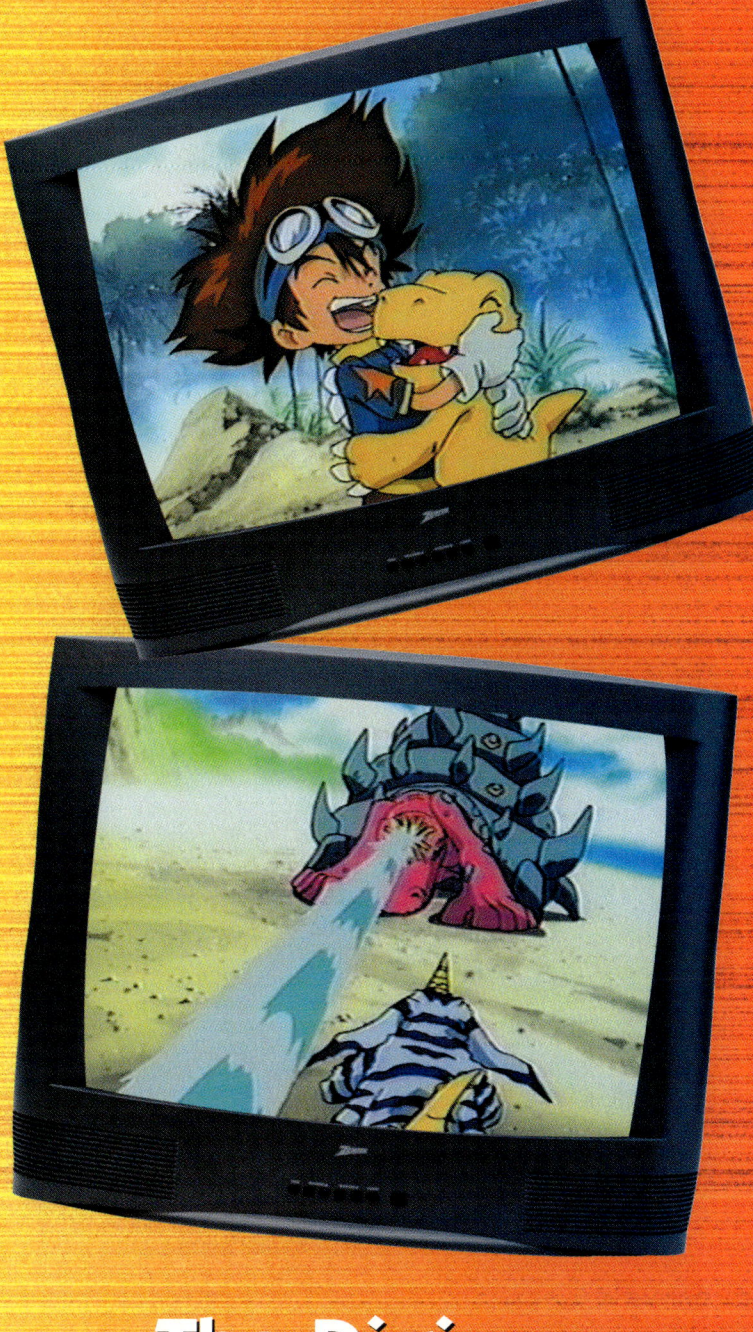

The Digimon are the kids' protectors in the often-dangerous Digiworld.

Episode 12: DigiBaby Boom
T.K. and Patamon are still on Infinity Mountain. There they find Primary Village, where all the Digimon are born. Patamon and Elecmon (the caretaker of the baby Digimon) get into a fight but eventually make up, and T.K. and Patamon rejoin the others.

Episode 13: The Legend of the DigiDestined
Devimon appears again to the children, this time as a huge version of himself. None of the Digimon is a match for him, so finally Patamon Digivolves into Angemon and is able to defeat Devimon. But Angemon used all his strength in the battle and reverts to an egg. Once Devimon is vanquished, a mysterious old man appears.

Episode 14: Departure for a New Continent
The old man, Gennai, tells the children of Tags and Crests that will enable their Digimon to Digivolve even further. He says they can search for them on the continent of Server. Leomon and the other good Digimon help the children build a raft, and they sail for Server — but on the ocean they're swallowed by Whamon. They destroy the Black Gear in Whamon's stomach and he shows them where their Tags are hidden.

Episode 15: The Dark Network of Etemon
Five days after they sail, the children reach Server, where they are attacked by new enemies, Etemon and Gazimon. Their Digimon are no match for Etemon, and the children realized that they need to Digivolve to a higher level to have a chance. Tai finds the Crest of Courage.

Episode 16: The Arrival of SkullGreymon
Impatient to have Agumon Digivolve, Tai forces him to eat and eat. When faced with an enemy Greymon sent by Etemon, Tai forces Agumon to evolve. But because Tai had forced Agumon to evolve when both were unready, Agumon evolves into SkullGreymon. Just as Skull Greymon is about to turn on the children, he uses up his strength and devolves into Koromon. Joe finds the Crest of Responsibility.

Episode 17: The Crest of Sincerity
As the party walks through the desert, it finds a huge cruise ship. Unfortunately, it's a trap set by Kokatorimon, another of Etemon's henchmen. Kokatorimon captures the boys and their Digimon, but Palmon and Biyomon save the day. Mimi finds the Crest of Sincerity.

Episode 18: The Pixiemon Cometh
An enemy Digimon attacks the children, but remembering what happened before, Tai is too scared to have Agumon evolve. Just in the nick of time, they're rescued by Pixiemon, who takes them to his hideout for training. Matt and Izzy slip away in the night to look for their Crests and find the Crests of Friendship and of Knowledge. Tai and Agumon renew their faith in themselves and Agumon is able to evolve again.

The DigiDestined are on a quest to rid the Digiworld of the evil Black Gears.

Episode 19: The Prisoner of the Pyramid

In the desert, T.K. finds the Crest of Hope. The children realize that the Digiworld is inside a computer network. This makes Tai cocky because he thinks, wrongly, that since it's not real he can't be hurt. Datamon kidnaps Sora in his plot for revenge against Etemon. Once Tai realizes that he's not invincible, he hesitates and is unable to save Sora.

Episode 20: The Earthquake of MetalGreymon

Tai saves Sora from Datamon and Sora finds her Crest. Datamon tries to destroy Etemon, but Etemon escapes and attacks the children. Agumon evolves into MetalGreymon and defeats Etemon, but he and Tai are swallowed up in a dimensional warp created by the battle.

Episode 21: Home Away from Home

Tai finds himself back in the real world. When he arrives home, he realizes that no time has passed since he has been in the Digiworld. Realizing that the problems in the Digiworld are having an effect on the real world, Tai and Agumon return to the Digiworld.

Episode 22: Forget About It!

When Tai and Agumon return to the Digiworld, they find Tokomon but not T.K. Tokomon tells them what has happened in their absence, including the fact that T.K. has left him to go off with a strange Digimon named DemiDevimon. Once T.K. realizes that he has been lied to, he joins up again with Tai, Agumon and Patamon.

Episode 23: Were Garurumon's Diner

Matt finds Joe and Gomamon being forced to work in a diner. Matt starts working there too, to help Joe, but DemiDevimon's plotting causes Matt to abandon Joe. Tai and T.K. find Matt and they realize what DemiDevimon has been doing. Gabumon Digivolves into WereGarurumon and defeats the owner of the diner. The children break into two groups to search for the others.

➡

Shellmon is the first Champion Digimon the kids encounter and defeat.

Digimon 51

The Digimon steadily Digivolve into more powerful forms.

Episode 24: No Questions, Please
Izzy and Tentomon are searching for Gennai when they are captured by Vademon. Izzy abandons his curiosity and becomes indifferent to anything that happens. Tentomon becomes so sad he devolves into Pabumon; only then does Izzy realize what he's done. Once Izzy gets back his curiosity, his Tag and his Crest, Tentomon is able to evolve into MegaKabuterimon and defeat Vademon. Gennai gives Izzy the Digimon Analyzer.

Episode 25: Princess Karaoke
Tai and Joe find Mimi in a castle belonging to the Gekomon and the Otamamon. These Digimon want Mimi to sing a song to revive their master, Shogun Gekomon, but Mimi acts like a spoiled brat instead. Realizing her selfishness, Mimi revives Shogun Gekomon, but he attacks the children instead of thanking them. It takes Metal Greymon's strength to defeat him.

Episode 26: Sora's Crest of Love
All the children are together again, except for Sora. DemiDevimon had convinced her that she was unworthy of the Crest of Love, and so she's reluctant to join the others. When she finally realizes that she is loved and able to love, Biyomon Digivolves into Garudamon.

Episode 27: The Gateway Home
Gennai once again appears to the children and tells them that Myotismon is planning to invade Earth in search of the eighth DigiDestined. They head to Myotismon's castle and battle DemiDevimon, Gatomon and DeviDramon, but the gate to Earth closes before their eyes.

Episode 28: It's All In the Cards
Gennai tells the children that they must use cards to open the gate to the real world. But there is one card too many, and Gennai does not know which one is the extra one. While fending off attacks from Myotismon's henchmen, Tai manages to get the cards in the right order and opens the gate to the real world. They find themselves back at the camp.

Episode 29: Return to Highton View Terrace
Pretending their Digimon are stuffed animals, the children make their way to Highton View Terrace, where they realize that four years ago they witnessed a battle between two Digimon here. Believing that this is the reason they were chosen as the DigiDestined, they conclude that the eighth child must also have seen the battle.

Greymon is the champion stage of Tai's evolved companion Digimon.

Episode 30: Almost Home Free

Since the eighth child was not at Highton View Terrace, the children decide he must be in Odaiba, and they try to make their way home. Without thinking, they use all their money on food and are left with no way home. While they try to figure out a way back, Sora's cousin drives by and offers them a ride. But Gesomon attacks them before they get far. Since the battle has already made such a scene, they give up any pretense of hiding their Digimon and use Ikkakumon to give them a ride home.

This is one of the most edited episodes. In the original Japanese version, instead of getting a ride from Sora's cousin, the children are hitchhiking and are picked up by a stranger.

Episode 31: The Eighth Digivice

The children return to their own homes and, although they realize no time has passed while they were in the Digiworld, they are very happy to see their families again. Gennai e-mails Izzy and tells him that another Digimon, Raremon, has appeared. Unable to reach anyone else, Izzy and Tentomon set out on their own. While out, Izzy's Digivice starts reacting, and he is convinced that the eighth DigiDestined must live nearby.

Episode 32: Gatomon Comes Calling

Deciding that the eighth child must also have lived in Highton View Terrace, the children get out their old address books and have Joe call everyone listed to see if anyone has moved. The other children split up and search the city. Back at the Kamiya residence, Gatomon finds Kari, but is unsure whether she is the eighth child.

Episode 33: Out On The Town

Matt and T.K. are taking the subway home when T.K. and Patamon get into a fight. Patamon gets off the train and the others follow in search of him. They meet Pumpkinmon and Gotsumon, two of Myotismon's henchmen who are more interested in having fun than in capturing the DigiDestined. This doesn't sit too well with Myotismon, though, and he sentences them to life in his dungeon. Patamon comes by and, seeing T.K. in danger, evolves into Angemon. Myotismon escapes and returns to his hideout.

In the original Japanese version, Pumpkinmon and Gotsumon were killed, not just sent to a dungeon.

Episode 34: The Eighth Child Revealed

Across the way from Kari's window Gatomon watches, still unable to decide what to do. Wizardmon finds the eighth Digivice and brings it to Gatomon. It jolts her into remembering her past. Realizing that Kari is indeed the eighth child and that she is her Digimon partner, Gatomon heads for Myotismon's hideout to reclaim Kari's lost Crest. Unfortunately, Myotismon realizes he's been betrayed and takes Gatomon hostage. ➜

The mighty Seadramon is so huge that the kids mistake him for an island.

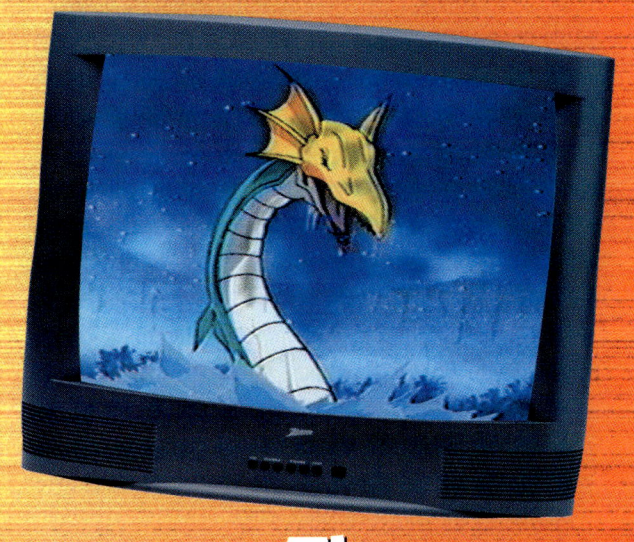

The challenges facing the kids grow more complex as their companions grow more powerful.

The kids' triumphs are soured by increasing squabbles within their group.

Episode 35: Flower Power
Seeing on a news broadcast that there is no communication with Odaiba because of the fog, T.K. decides to find Matt. Joe is also trying to get back to Odaiba, and when he meets up with T.K., they use Ikkakumon to get across the bay. Myotismon captures Mimi and her family, and Palmon evolves into Lillymon to save them from Dark Tyranomon.

Episode 36: City Under Siege
Birdramon takes the injured Lillymon and escapes along with Sora. Tai leaves Kari with Matt and goes to find the hostages. He meets up with Sora and tells her to find Matt and Kari. Meanwhile, T.K. and Joe are attacked by Mega Seadramon. Ikkakumon Digivolves into Zudomon and saves the day. Back in Odaiba, Kari turns herself into Myotismon's henchman, saying she doesn't want anyone else to get hurt because of her.

Episode 37: Wizardmon's Gift
The children all meet up at the TV station, along with Matt's dad. Wizardmon tells them about Kari and Gatomon. With Matt's dad showing them the way, they come to the place where Kari is being held by Myotismon. With her Crest and Digivice finally in hand, Kari is able to make Gatomon evolve into Angewomon. Angewomon defeats Myotismon, but the mysterious fog remains.

Episode 38: Prophecy
Izzy receives an e-mail from Gennai telling them of an ancient prophecy regarding Myotismon. Believing they had defeated him already, the children give it little thought. But soon things start happening just like the prophecy foretold, and Myotismon is revived as Venom Myotismon. Izzy finds out that Venom Myotismon is at a previously unknown level: Mega. With help from Angemon and Angewomon, Agumon and Gabumon are able to warp-evolve to Mega too, becoming WereGreymon and Metal Garurumon.

Episode 39: The Battle for Earth
The other Digimon Digivolve and join the fight against Venom Myotismon. With their combined strength they are finally able to defeat him. Once he's gone the fog clears, but everything is not back to normal. Floating in the sky is a huge landmass, the Digiworld. Myotismon's prisoners awake and the children are reunited with their parents, but only for a short time. They know they must return to the Digiworld.

Episode 40: Enter the Dark Masters
Arriving in the Digiworld, the children look up and realize they can see the real world in the sky, just as they could see the Digiworld in the sky from Earth. They meet Chuumon, who tells them how the Dark Masters have taken over and rebuilt the Digiworld with Spiral Mountain as its center. The Dark Masters attack, but the children are saved at the last minute by Pixiemon, who holds them off while the children make their escape.

Episode 41: Seasick and Tired

The children find themselves back on the beach at File Island. They head for a shack on the beach, but Mimi and Joe are separated from the others. The other children are attacked by Scorpiomon. The captured children are saved at the last minute by Lillymon and Zudomon, who defeat Scorpiomon. Unfortunately, they still aren't strong enough to stand up to Metal Seadramon, and it looks like they might lose this one.

Episode 42: Under Pressure

The children are saved by Whamon, but Metal Seadramon sends his Divermon to search the ocean for them. Izzy finds out that WereGreymon's weapons are called Dramon Destroyers, meaning they are particularly effective against Dramon-type Digimon like Metal Seadramon. When they finally emerge from the ocean they find Metal Seadramon waiting for them, and WereGreymon battles him.

The following episodes have not yet aired in North America, so the titles will most likely be changed. Some Digimon names may change, too.

Episode 43: Puppetmon's Dangerous Game

The children defeat Metal Seadramon and head into the forest. As they get further in, they notice the ground below them has turned into a conveyor belt and is moving forward. Soon, even stranger things start happening. The children begin disappearing one by one until only Matt and T.K. are left. With the others out of the way, Puppetmon kidnaps T.K. and takes him to his mansion. But when Puppetmon isn't looking, T.K. manages to escape and free the others.

Episode 44: Jureimon and the Forest of Delusion

Seeing T.K. able to take care of himself, Matt becomes depressed, thinking that his little brother doesn't need him anymore. Matt and Gabumon leave the group to travel on their own. In the forest they meet Jureimon, who tells them that Matt must defeat his rival, Tai, to become the person he wants to be. Meanwhile, the other children are busy battling Puppetmon's henchmen. Matt and Gabumon return to where the others are and, with Gabumon Digivolved to Metal Garurumon, challenge Tai and Agumon to a duel.

Episode 45: Clash of the TwoMegas! WereGreymon vs. Metal Garurumon

At first Tai and Agumon don't want to fight, but seeing they have no choice, Agumon Digivolves into WereGreymon. In the middle of the fight, Hikari's body is taken over by an unknown presence. This presence speaks to the children, telling them about the Digiworld and why they were chosen to be the DigiDestined. Tai and Matt ➜

The kids return safely to the real world, only to discover the evil Digimon have followed them home.

With the help of new allies, the DigiDestined take on the evil Digimon.

make up, but Matt still decides to travel alone. Not wanting to see any more fighting, Mimi stays behind. Joe stays with her to try and convince her to rejoin the group.

Episode 46: Metal Etemon Strikes Back
The rest of the children head for Puppetmon's mansion. Mimi and Joe find an unconscious Ogremon who, once he comes to, decides to join them after seeing their kindness in tending to his wounds. Puppetmon attacks them but is distracted by Metal Etemon. The children escape.

Episode 47: The Wind! The Light! Saber Leomon
Joe and Mimi meet up with Leomon, who Digivolved into Saber Leomon while they were gone from the Digiworld. They arrive at the restaurant where Joe and Matt were forced to work. Metal Etemon appears again and battles Leomon. He is defeated, but Leomon is fatally wounded, too. Before he dies, he tells the children that he will be reborn in Primary Village. Meanwhile, the other children were doing their best against Puppetmon, but it looked like a losing battle until Metal Garurumon appeared and defeated the evil Digimon.

Episode 48: Machine Dragon's Bomb Attack!
Kari has a relapse of her cold, so Izzy and Tai go out looking for medicine. Machine Dramon is able to locate them through Izzy's computer and sends his Metal Empire Army after them. Once Izzy realizes how they are being located, he uses a program that hides their location. Unfortunately, Machine Dramon is not easily discouraged and simply begins bombing the whole area. The children fall into a huge pit and are separated.

Episode 49: Farewell, Numemon
Kari, T.K. and Sora find themselves in a huge sewer and search for the others. But instead of Izzy and Tai, they find WereMonzaemon, who is acting as a slave driver over a bunch of Numemon. Kari and Gatomon free the Numemon while the other Digimon attempt to distract WereMonzaemon. Although they're tired, Kari's light revives them, and they defeat the evil Digimon and continue to search for Tai and Izzy. The children are reunited, but Machine Dramon finds them and attacks. Agumon Digivolves into WereGreymon and defeats Machine Dramon.

Episode 50: A Woman's Battle! Lady Devimon
After defeating Machine Dramon, the children find the castle of the last of the Dark Masters. There they are faced with Lady Devimon, and the Digimon Digivolve one after another. Knowing that all their strength will be needed for the battle with Piedmon, Tai sends Sora and T.K. to search for Matt and the others.

Meanwhile, Mimi and Joe arrive at the ruins of Primary Village and are saddened to find many Digimon turned to stone. There they met Elecmon, who had found Matt's harmonica on the beach. Joe decides to follow Matt and, with Gomamon, sets off across the sea. Back at the castle, Lady Devimon is finally defeated and Piedmon appears.

Episode 51: Piedmon, Hell's Fool

Tai and the others finally arrive at Piedmon's castle on top of Spiral Mountain. Meanwhile, Matt and Gabumon are wandering in a dark cave created by the darkness in Matt's heart. But with Gabumon's encouragement, Matt realizes his true feelings and the cave disappears. Matt is reunited with Joe, but as they head for Spiral Mountain they find T.K., who tells them that Sora has fallen into a cave — the same cave that Matt had been in.

When the others persuade her that she doesn't have to be responsible for everything, Sora's negative feelings disappear, and so does the cave. They hurry back to the castle to find an injured Tai and WereGreymon fighting Piedmon. Matt's Crest of Friendship brings them back from the brink of death, and the two Megas attack the enemy.

Episode 52: The Holy Warrior, MagnaAngemon

Just when all the Digimon are attacking, Piedmon brings out a white handkerchief and turns Tai, Matt, WereGreymon and Metal Garurumon into dolls. The other children run away, but they can't escape Piedmon. One after the other, they are turned into dolls until only T.K. and Kari remain. Just when T.K. is about to give up hope, the doll of Matt which he has been holding encourages him to keep fighting.

His Crest of Hope glows and Angemon Digivolves into Magna Angemon and revives the other children and Digimon. Magna Angemon defeats Piedmon, but before they can begin celebrating, the children receive an e-mail from Gennai informing them that the Dark Masters were not the true threat to the Digiworld.

Episode 53: The Final Battle

The children fall into an endless world of darkness. All the negative energy coalesces into one being and it comes at them, using the attacks of all the Digimon the children had fought in the past. The Digimon devolve and the children lose their tags and crests. Then, everyone is broken down into data. The children are at a loss, but the Digimon encourage them and they regain hope. Their chests begin to glow with the shapes of their crests and the Digimon Digivolve to their highest forms. Before their eyes is the enemy Digimon.

Episode 54: The End of Summer

It seems they have defeated the evil Digimon, but with his dying breath he threatens to take the whole world with him. Determined not to give up, the children fight on, and their crests seal the enemy, saving the world from destruction. Although the children wish to stay longer in the Digiworld, Gennai tells them that unless they return home now they will be erased during the reconstruction of the Digiworld. Saying goodbye to their Digimon, the children return home. **Digimon**

The kids finally defeat the threat to both worlds after chasing their enemies back to the Digiworld.

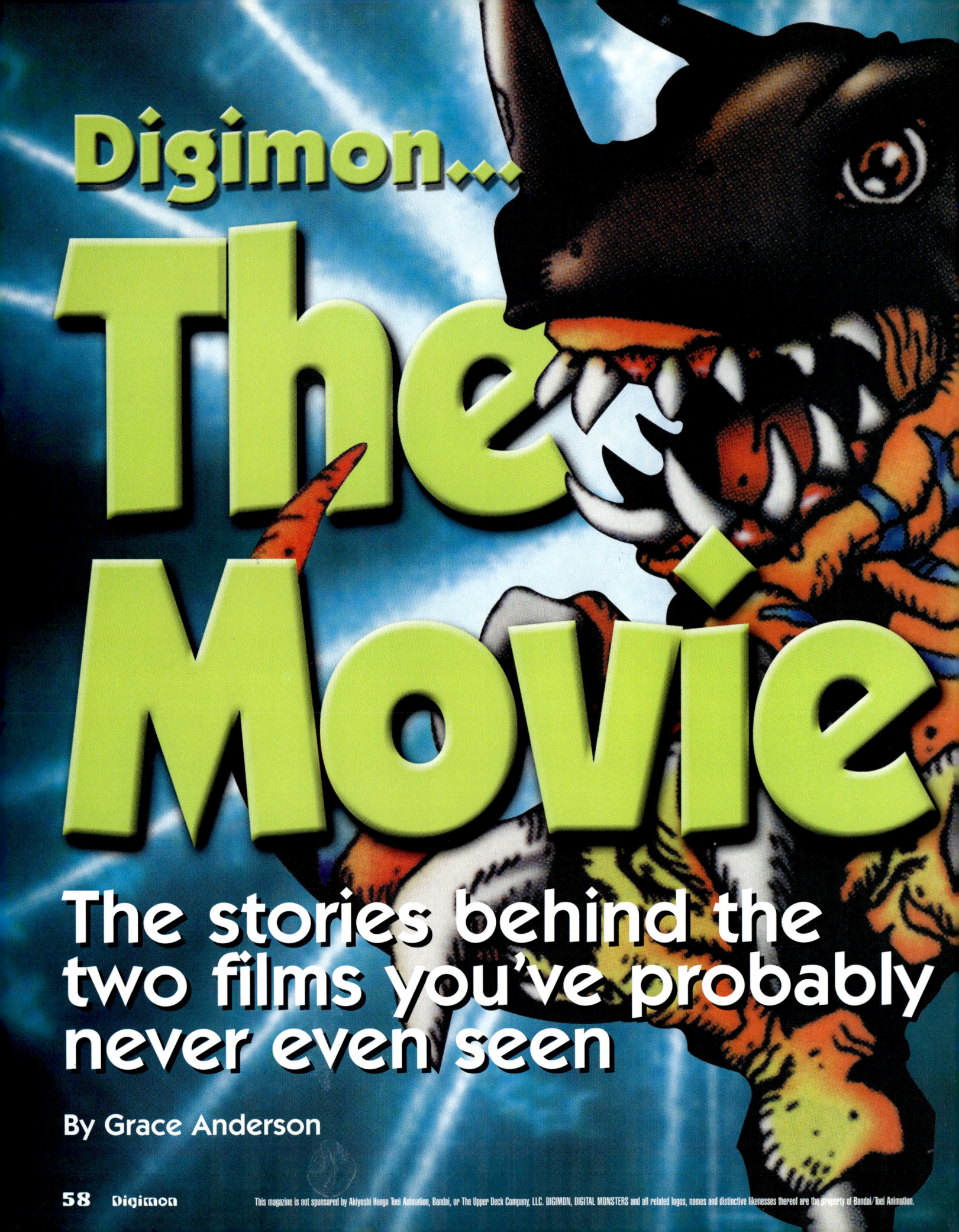

Digimon... The Movie

The stories behind the two films you've probably never even seen

By Grace Anderson

If you've ever wished that each episode of *Digimon Adventures* could just keep going on and on, or that a storyline could extend beyond a 30-minute episode, you're in luck. In addition to the TV series, there are two Digimon movies out in Japan.

The first, simply titled *Digimon: The Movie,* premiered last spring and is available on video. Only 20 minutes long, it was shown along with several other animated shorts in the theater. The second movie, *Our War Game,* is 40 minutes long and opened March 4.

Both movies have been picked up by Saban for North American release, but no release date is known. A theatrical release is unlikely because the combined running time of both movies is only about an hour. My best guess is a direct-to-video release, but they might also be shown as TV movies.

Although it takes place only six months after the end of the TV series, the children (in the movie) look years older.

The movies' animation style takes some getting used to. Many who have seen screen shots have commented on how much better they like the look of the TV animation compared to the movies. The character design makes the children look quite different. This is especially noticeable in the second movie; although it takes place only six months after the end of the TV series, the children look years older. But it's not only the character designs that have changed; the backgrounds are very realistic, almost photographic.

What the second movie has that the TV series and the first movie don't is some very high-quality computer animation — not the kind seen in the transformation sequences of WereGarurumon and MetalGreymon in the TV series, but anime-style CGI that blends better with the traditional cel animation. →

Digimon... The Movie?

The First Adventure

The first movie centers around the happenings at Highton View Terrace four years before the children's first trip to the Digiworld. In episode 29 of the TV series, the children remember that it was then that they first saw the Digimon. The movie serves as an extended flashback told from Tai's point of view.

One night he wakes up to go to the bathroom and finds Kari staring at a glowing Digi-egg on the computer screen. Before their eyes the egg begins to emerge from the screen. The next morning the egg hatches and out pops a strange black little animal. It's a Digi-baby — Botamon to be precise, but of course the children don't know that. He soon Digivolves again into Koromon and later that night into Agumon.

But this isn't the same Agumon we have all come to love from the TV series; this is a much bigger, meaner Agumon. With Kari on his back, Agumon jumps out the window. Not bothering to change his pajamas, Tai rushes out the front door in hot pursuit.

Suddenly, the sky opens up and another Digimon appears. It's a huge, green bird-type Digimon, Parrotmon. He and Agumon battle and eventually Agumon Digivolves once more, this time becoming an even larger dinosaur, Greymon. Greymon manages to destroy the giant bird, but to Kari's dismay the dinosaur disappears, too, and the movie ends with Kari calling after her lost friend, "Koromon! Koromon!"

This is a cute movie, but nothing really new if you've been watching the TV series. ➜

Digimon... The Movie?

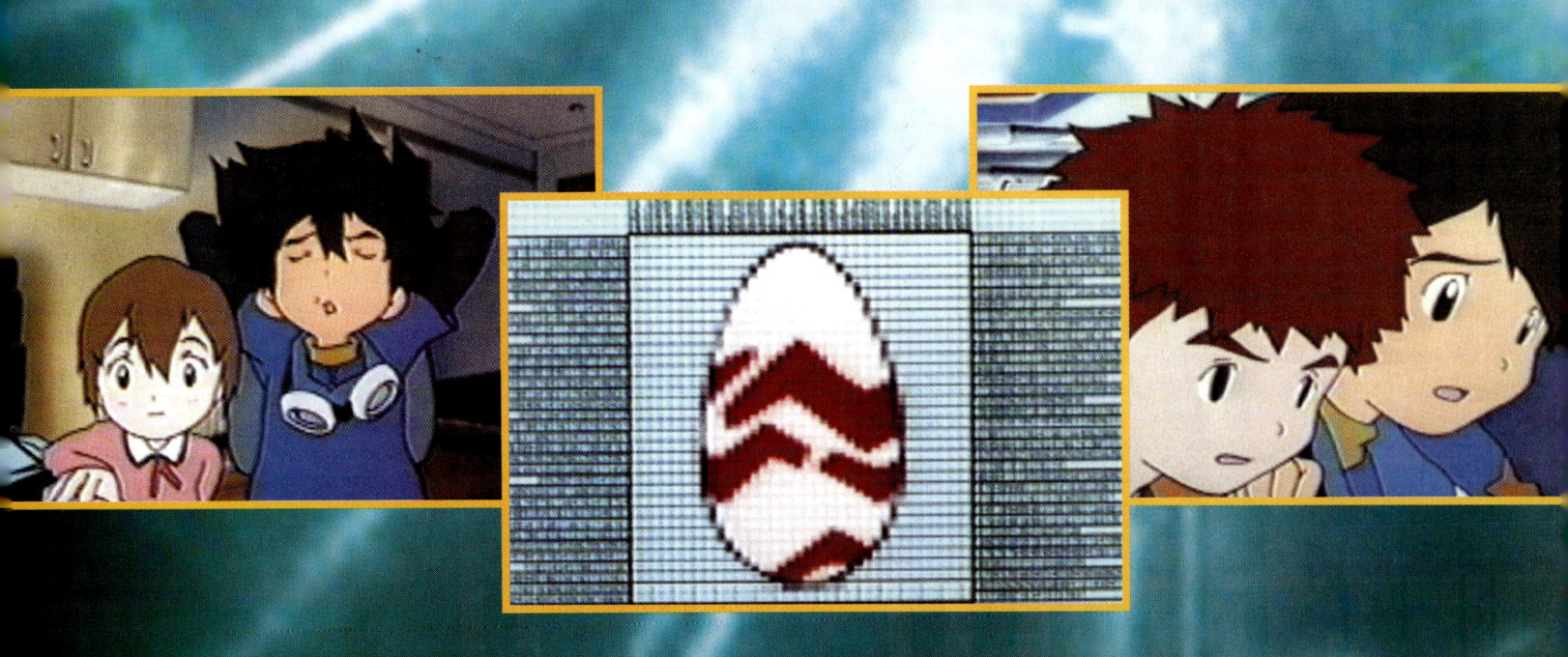

One night (Tai) finds Kari staring at a glowing Digi-egg on the computer screen.

The Adventure Continues

The second movie takes places six months after the children have returned home from the Digimon world. It is now spring vacation instead of summer and the children are all busy. Mimi and her family are in Hawaii, Joe is taking entrance exams for junior high, Kari is going to a birthday party, and Matt and T.K. are visiting their grandma in the country. The only ones not doing anything are Tai, Izzy and Sora.

While playing on his computer, Izzy sees what seems to be a Digi-egg appear on his screen and hatch into a small jellyfish-like Digimon. Realizing that this can't be a good thing, Izzy hurries over to Tai's house to tell him about it. Once there he hooks up his laptop to Tai's computer and shows him the Digimon. Before their eyes it Digivolves once more. Tai tries calling the others, but finds no one is home. He asks Izzy to call Sora for him, but Sora is still upset at Tai over a silly argument they had the other day and tells her mom to say she's not home. ➔

Digimon... The Movie?

In the second movie, an evil Digimon invades computers around the world, eating data and causing confusion.

Just when it looks like there is nothing they can do against this Digimon, Izzy gets an e-mail from Gennai. Gennai tells him that he will transfer Tentomon and Agumon into their computer to fight the evil Digimon. But the Digimon Digivolves again and is too strong for the two to defeat him. Izzy looks at his computer and finds e-mail from other children around the world who have been watching the battle. Some send words of encouragement, others only derision. The Digimon makes his way into various computer systems around the world, eating the data and causing confusion wherever he goes. Tai finally gets a hold of Matt and T.K., but the two boys are hard-pressed to find a computer in the small village in which their grandma lives.

After what seems forever, they find a computer, and Gennai sends Patamon and Gabumon to help out the other two. Agumon and Gabumon Warp Digivolve into War-Greymon and MetalGarurumon, but still it's no use; this →

Digimon....
The Movie?

Izzy enlists the aid of children around the world to stop the evil Digimon.

Digimon is stronger than anything they've ever seen before. The evil Digimon starts a countdown, and Izzy receives e-mail from a boy who tells them that when the timer reaches zero, missiles will be fired all over the world.

Just when it looks like there is no hope left, Matt and Tai somehow find a way into the computer and revive their Digimon. WarGreymon and MetalGarurumon join together into one huge Digimon but are still unable to catch the enemy. Then Izzy has an idea: If he forwards all the e-mail from the children watching to the address of the evil Digimon, he might be able to slow him down. His plan works and the children are able to strike a fatal blow at the Digimon. With one second left, the world is saved.

The second movie is more exciting than the first, but both are enjoyable, and fans of the TV series will definitely want to see them. Hopefully, we'll be able to see the North American versions of these sometime soon. **Digimon**

Digi-Mall

Malls and retail outlets all across the country are exploding with Digimon toys. Find your favorite Digimon monsters transformed into stuff you can wear, play with, challenge your friends to a battle with or even use to express your creative side.

Everything from high-tech electronic Digivice games to old-fashioned coloring and activity books are filling store shelves. So, it won't be too hard to find many of these products at stores near you!

Interactive Digivice Game
A portable LCD game that lets kids partner with their favorite Digimon characters to battle and collect other Digimon as they walk through an amazing adventure. Connect with a friend's Digivice for hand-to-hand combat. By Bandai.
Suggested retail: $12.99 each

Digimon Talking Figures

These Digimon can actually speak. Agumon, Gabumon and Patamon say phrases from the hit Fox Kids television series. By Bandai.
Suggested retail: $5.99 each

Action Feature Digimon
Each rough-and-tough, 2.5-inch action figure comes with a collectible sticker and mini poster. The highly detailed Digimon have their own unique action feature, such as Meramon with fire-throwing action and Patamon with flapping wings. By Bandai.
Suggested retail: $2.99 each

Digimon dX
Extreme dX mini skateboards have just been taken to another level. Each board comes with a 1.5-inch Digimon figure key chain, finger bindings and a display stand. Series one, two and three will offer 36 cool board designs. By Bandai.
Suggested retail: $4.99 each

70 Digimon   This magazine is not sponsored by Akiyoshi Hongo Toei Animation, Bandai, or The Upper Deck Company, LLC. DIGIMON, DIGITAL MONSTERS and all related logos, names and distinctive likenesses thereof are the property of Bandai/Toei Animation.

Digimon Backpack

Take Agumon or Biyomon on the road with you. Each Digimon backpack is made of plush fabric and has adjustable straps and a zipper compartment. By Bandai.
Suggested retail: $14.99 each

Collectible Digimon Sets

Each set contains four to six 1.5-inch Digimon figures in a different "digivolved" stage. A two-sided poster featuring the stars of Digimon is included. Other sets are available, too. By Bandai.
Suggested retail: $4.99 a set

72 Digimon   This magazine is not sponsored by Akiyoshi Hongo Toei Animation, Bandai, or The Upper Deck Company, LLC. DIGIMON, DIGITAL MONSTERS and all related logos, names and distinctive likenesses thereof are the property of Bandai/Toei Animation.

Digivolving Action Figures

"Digivolve" these 5-inch action figures to the next level of strength and power. Kabuterimon, Greymon, Garurumon, Patamon and Birdramon can be magically transformed right before your eyes. Each Digimon comes with a unique trading card and poster. By Bandai.
Suggested retail: $7.99 each

This magazine is not sponsored by Akiyoshi Hongo Toei Animation, Bandai, or The Upper Deck Company, LLC. DIGIMON, DIGITAL MONSTERS and all related logos, names and distinctive likenesses thereof are the property of Bandai/Toei Animation.

Digimon 73

Sticker Activity Books

Thrilling full color stickers make the challenging puzzles and games in this book even more exciting. Connect the dots, solve mazes and color all the pages. By Honey Bear Books. **Suggested retail: $2.49 each**

Deluxe Micro Playset

These playsets include one character and one Digimon that Digivolves from Rookie level to Champion. Agumon Digivolves to Greymon, Gabumon to Garurumon and Tentomon to Kabuterimon. By Bandai. **Suggested retail: $9.99 a set**

Giant Coloring and Activity Books

Join in the Digimon fun with cool coloring scenes, puzzles, mazes and more. Loaded with hours and hours of fun. By Honey Bear Books.
Suggested retail: $1.79 each

Digimon 75

Jumbo Magnets
Collect all 13 of these extra-large magnets. Great to stick on the fridge. Find Tai & Agumon, Mimi & Palmon, Greymon, Garurumon and more. By Fun4All.
Suggested retail: $2.99 each

76 Digimon

Lenticular Digimon Buttons

Watch Digimon evolve multiple times on these special buttons from Japan. Wear them on your backpack, jacket or anywhere. By Banpresto.

Digimon Video: Volume 1

Catch the coolest kids and craziest creatures in the whole wide digital world with Digimon. Meet Tai, Sora, Matt, T.K., Izzy, Mimi and Joe — seven young friends who team up with a colorful assortment of "monsters" to battle evil forces in the ultimate digital adventure. Seven collectible cards included. By Fox Kids Video. **Suggested retail: $9.99**

Collectible Digimon Cards

Three sets of Collectible Digimon cards have been released. Each set comes with eight cards per pack, including six character cards, one checklist card and one collectors foil chase card. By Bandai. **Suggested retail: $1.99 a pack**

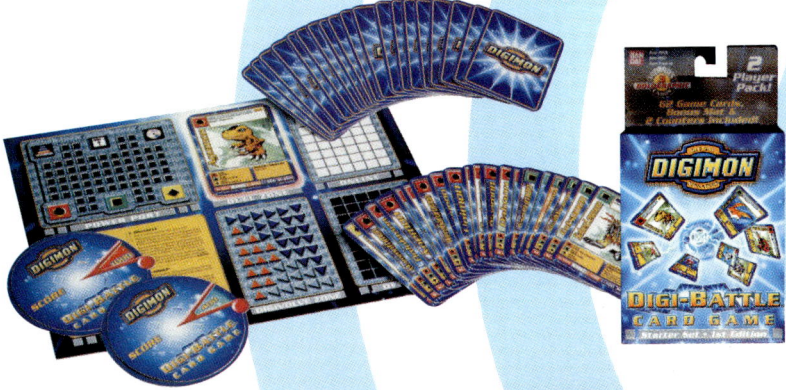

Digi-Battle Game Cards

Each Digi-Battle Game Card starter set contains all the elements for a two-player game. The set includes a play-mat, point counters, 14 option cards, one bonus foil card, 48 Digimon cards, which include two foil bonus holographic cards. By Bandai. **Suggested retail: $9.99 a set**

japanime.com

much more than a store—we're your friend in japan

It's time to get some Digimon!

www.japanime.com/digimon.html

**Trading cards
Plush toys
Videos**

Always in stock!

Visit us at www.japanime.com   Contact us at sales@japanime.com   Dealer inquiries welcome

SECURE SERVER—ALL MAJOR CREDIT CARDS—EXPRESS MAIL SHIPPING DIRECT FROM JAPAN

80 Digimon This magazine is not sponsored by Akiyoshi Hongo, Toei Animation, Bandai, or The Upper Deck Company, LLC. DIGIMON, DIGITAL MONSTERS and all related logos, names and distinctive likenesses thereof are the property of Bandai/Toei Animation.

Can't Collect Just Digi-One

Better narrow your focus before you go gonzo

By Gordon Kane

SO YOU WANT TO COLLECT DIGIMON toys. Do you know what's available? Where to find it? What it will cost? And do you know what area of Digimon you're going to concentrate on? Action figures? Plushes? Trading cards? Japanese-only? English-only? Or are you a gonzo collector that has to have it all?

When it comes to collecting Digimon, today's wired society has a plethora of options at its disposal. The Internet is my primary source of researching, inquiring about, locating, requesting and purchasing Digimon items.

Usenet newsgroups are an excellent source of information. They're full of questions that people have asked (which are probably similar to those you might ask) and answers to those questions. If no one else has asked your specific question, feel free to post it. If your ISP hasn't given you a method to access newsgroups, try Web portals like www.remarq.com and www.deja.com/usenet.

Another good source of information is targeted e-mail lists. Many Web portals host e-mail lists (one that springs to mind is www.onelist.com). Often before joining a list you can browse an archive of prior messages to determine if it has sufficient activity, maturity and depth of knowledge. Joining these lists helps you establish contacts with people with similar interests in countries other than the United States.

The key to collecting Japanese Digimon items is knowing what's available. The manufacturer's site is a good place to start. Bandai Japan (www.bandai.co.jp) has lots of pictures and even a Digimon Channel for all the Digi-maniacs (www.digimon.channel.or.jp). The pictures come in handy when you've made contact with someone who doesn't have a comprehensive grasp of the Japanese alphabet.

I often browse eBay (www.ebay.com) for items that are similar to what I'm looking for, then send the seller an e-mail. You meet other collectors this way as well as people who own toy stores. And some of my best contacts have been U.S. military personnel stationed in Japan. →

Deluxe Plush
These 12-inch Digimon are in Champion mode. Find Garurumon, Ikkakumon, Togemon and Greymon. By Bandai. **Suggested retail: $14.99 each**

Bean Bag Plush
Six-inch Digimon characters can be found in furry, plush Digivolved form: Agumon, Biyomon, Gabumon, Gomamon, Palmon, Patamon, Tentomon, Tsunomon and Koromon. By Bandai. **Suggested retail: $5.99 a set**

Digivolving Garurumon
Transform Garurumon into WereGarurumon with this fully articulated action figure. Digivolving Greymon, Patamon and Birdramon are also available in the series. By Bandai. **Suggested retail: $14.99 each**

82 Digimon

This magazine is not sponsored by Akiyoshi Hongo Toei Animation, Bandai, or The Upper Deck Company, LLC. DIGIMON, DIGITAL MONSTERS and all related logos, names and distinctive likenesses thereof are the property of Bandai/Toei Animation.

One of the main factors that will determine where you look is the type of collecting you want to do. Virtual-pet collectors need to focus their searches and inquiries on the Japanese marketplace. Stuffed-animal collectors may get a domestic avenue to pursue. But right now, all the available plushes and bean bags are Japanese.

Action-figure collectors have it a little easier. The current Bandai-made sets (numbered I, II, III, IV, V, VI and VII) are the same as the Japanese assortments, which were themselves merely repackaged assortments from the cage sets that hit the market when Digimon first became hot in Japan.

The U.S. has yet to see the WereGreymon and Metal Garurumon transformers, but I suspect they'll be over here soon. These transforming figures are the same ones that are being sold in Japan at significantly higher prices. (I'm surprised these figures are retailing for less than $15 in the U.S.)

There is also a line of 2.5-inch figures that features eight more figures than I've seen offered in Japan. The Gabumon, Agumon and Patamon figures from this line have plastic Digivices that are not found in the Japanese packages. ➜

Action Feature Digimon
Each 2.5-inch action figure comes with a collectible sticker and mini poster. The highly detailed Digimon have their own unique action feature, such as Meramon with fire-throwing action and Patamon with flapping wings. By Bandai. **Suggested retail: $2.99 each**

Collectible Digimon Sets
Each set contains four to six 1.5-inch Digimon figures in different Digivolved staged. A two-sided poster featuring the stars of Digimon is included. By Bandai. **Suggested retail: $4.99 a set**

Snap-Together Digimodels
Creating killer likenesses of Birdramon, WereGarurumon, MetalGreymon and MegaKabuterimon is a snap with these detailed plastic models. Each model also includes a sticker sheet for adding details such as eyes and stripes. By Bandai. **Suggested retail: $4.99 each**

Cards, Cards, Cards!

Card collectors can collect Japanese-only or English-only cards or try to hunt down every card created. There are at least two sets of Japanese cards featuring shots from the animated series as well as at least two Japanese card games featuring the Digimon creatures.

In North America, Upper Deck has released a trading-card series and a game-card series. There are 34 cards in the trading card set, 62 cards in the game-card starter set and 54 cards in the Series 1 booster set. Series 2 game cards will add another 54 cards to the pool, and if the English version follows the Japanese game, another starter set and an additional booster series should follow.

Collectors of character-specific items featuring the Digi-Destined don't have much with which to work. I'm not aware of anything available in Japan, although the most recent Toy Fair did show some action figures featuring the kids.

Collectors of specific Digimon can expect levels of success and selections of products that vary wildly from creature to creature. Fans of Agumon, Patamon and Gabumon have many options. Gomamon, Tentomon, Palmon and Biyomon have fewer options. Fans of monsters like Snimon, Skull Greymon or Metal Seadramon might find a trading card or some other items sporting their favorite character, but it's unlikely they will find that character available in every type of toy.

If you decide to concentrate on Japanese Digimon items, the best method is the most expensive: visit Japan. But seeing how that breaks most budgets and leaves no money for toys, you probably ought to pursue other options that only require patience and an investment of your free time. ➤

Super Bromaido and Digi-Battle Trading Card Games

Japan is home to not one, but two Digimon trading-card games, Super Bromaido and Digi-Battle. Both are available in starter decks and boosters.
Suggested retail: $14.95 a deck

Card Tactics Electronic Card Game

It's an electronic game. It's a card game. It's Card Tactics! Battle your favorite Digimon against a friend by inputting data from the included trading cards into your calculator-size Digivice and linking up. By Bandai.
Suggested retail: $59.95

Hexa-plate System Hybrid Game

The Hexa-Plate System is an all-new hybrid of the Digimon card game and a board game. It comes with 82 cards with fronts and backs different from standard Digimon cards, small hexagonal game boards and tiny rubber Digimon game pieces. A rule book is also included but, unfortunately, it's only in Japanese. By Bandai. **Suggested retail: $34.95**

Mini Digimon Figures

These 1-inch Digimon figures are strikingly similar to the ones Pokémon fans have been collecting. They even include the same candy pellets. Yum! By Bandai. **Suggested retail: $1.99 each**

Problems associated with collecting Japanese items often arise, even if you never leave home. First, the search for a precise item can take weeks or months. Second, imported items cost more, so if the toy you buy is released in America, you may have paid more for it just to have it six months before anyone else. When buying Japanese items directly from Japanese sources, you are buying them sight-unseen, and if you're a real stickler for mint packaging, you might be upset with what you get.

Pursuit of domestically released toys requires its own brand of patience. If the toy is really hot, you'll either have to wait until there's a quantity on the shelf that lasts more than a day, or else you need to learn the days your favorite store gets its toy deliveries. Some collectors have even enlisted the help of a store employee (or gone into retailing themselves) to ensure they get their collections completed as quickly as possible.

Competition for domestic items may be fierce initially, making them hard to find, but the supply soon turns plentiful. So there's no need to fight over a purchase or resort to hiding the toy from other prospective buyers. Import toys, on the other hand, require you to be constantly on the lookout, and you have to be ready to post your best bid right at the beginning. Often there are no steals or great deals to be found, and this might be your only chance to get the item for a long period of time. (Then again, one could show up locally the next day.)

Choose, bid and spend wisely, and you'll complete your collection in no time. Happy collecting! **Digimon**

Digimon Card Lineup & Price Guide

Because the 62 cards in this set were released in complete-set form only, pricing on singles remained consistent in the weeks following its initial release. With the release of the booster sets, the prices of certain cards in this set are subject to change as players learn how these cards interact with those in the booster sets. Note also that to complete a set consisting of only base-set cards (as compared to a set combining base-set and holographic cards), it was necessary to buy two or more sets or purchase or trade for individual cards. This accounts for the wider variations in base-set pricing.

Digi-Battle Card Game

Starter Set/First Edition
(Gaming Cards, Upper Deck)

Starter Box (62):	$10-15
Base Set (62):	$8-16
Parallel Holographic Set (62):	$50-75
Parallel Holographic Singles:	$1-2

Agumon

Card #: ST-1
Type: Rookie
Value: $0.10-0.25

Greymon

Card #: ST-2
Type: Champion
Value: $0.10-0.25

Biyomon

Card #: ST-3
Type: Rookie
Value: $0.10-0.25

Birdramon

Card #: ST-4
Type: Champion
Value: $0.10-0.25

This magazine is not sponsored by Akiyoshi Hongo, Toei Animation, Bandai, or The Upper Deck Company, LLC. DIGIMON, DIGITAL MONSTERS and all related logos, names and distinctive likenesses thereof are the property of Bandai/Toei Animation.

Gabumon

Card #: **ST-5**
Type: **Rookie**
Value: **$0.10-0.25**

Garurumon

Card #: **ST-6**
Type: **Champion**
Value: **$0.10-0.25**

Tentomon

Card #: **ST-7**
Type: **Rookie**
Value: **$0.10-0.25**

Kabuterimon

Card #: **ST-8**
Type: **Champion**
Value: **$0.10-0.25**

Palmon

Card #: **ST-9**
Type: **Rookie**
Value: **$0.10-0.25**

Togemon

Card #: **ST-10**
Type: **Champion**
Value: **$0.10-0.25**

Gomamon

Card #: ST-11
Type: Rookie
Value: $0.10-0.25

Ikkakumon

Card #: ST-12
Type: Champion
Value: $0.10-0.25

Patamon

Card #: ST-13
Type: Rookie
Value: $0.10-0.25

Angemon

Card #: ST-14
Type: Champion
Value: $0.10-0.25

Nanimon

Card #: ST-15
Type: Champion
Value: $0.10-0.25

Unimon

Card #: ST-16
Type: Champion
Value: $0.10-0.25

Centarumon

Card #: ST-17
Type: Champion
Value: $0.10-0.25

Kunemon

Card #: ST-18
Type: Rookie
Value: $0.10-0.25

Dokugumon

Card #: ST-19
Type: Champion
Value: $0.10-0.25

Musyamon

Card #: ST-20
Type: Champion
Value: $0.10-0.25

Kimeramon

Card #: ST-21
Type: Ultimate
Value: $0.10-0.25

Rockmon

Card #: ST-22
Type: Champion
Value: $0.10-0.25

Gotsumon
Card #: ST-23
Type: Rookie
Value: $0.10-0.25

Otamamon
Card #: ST-24
Type: Rookie
Value: $0.10-0.25

Tortomon
Card #: ST-25
Type: Champion
Value: $0.10-0.25

Starmon
Card #: ST-26
Type: Champion
Value: $0.10-0.25

Gekomon
Card #: ST-27
Type: Champion
Value: $0.10-0.25

MegaKabuterimon
Card #: ST-28
Type: Ultimate
Value: $0.10-0.25

Triceramon

Card #: ST-29
Type: Ultimate
Value: $0.10-0.25

Piximon

Card #: ST-30
Type: Ultimate
Value: $0.10-0.25

Okuwamon

Card #: ST-31
Type: Ultimate
Value: $0.10-0.25

SkullGreymon

Card #: ST-32
Type: Ultimate
Value: $0.10-0.25

HerculesKabuterimon

Card #: ST-33
Type: Mega
Value: $0.10-0.25

SaberLeomon

Card #: ST-34
Type: Mega
Value: $0.10-0.25

Dolphmon

Card #: ST-35
Type: Champion
Value: $0.10-0.25

Coelamon

Card #: ST-36
Type: Champion
Value: $0.10-0.25

Octomon

Card #: ST-37
Type: Champion
Value: $0.10-0.25

Zudomon

Card #: ST-38
Type: Ultimate
Value: $0.10-0.25

MarineDevimon

Card #: ST-39
Type: Ultimate
Value: $0.10-0.25

Pukumon

Card #: ST-40
Type: Mega
Value: $0.10-0.25

Digimon **93**

Candlemon

Card #: ST-41
Type: Rookie
Value: $0.10-0.25

DemiDevimon

Card #: ST-42
Type: Rookie
Value: $0.10-0.25

Apemon

Card #: ST-43
Type: Champion
Value: $0.10-0.25

Wizardmon

Card #: ST-44
Type: Champion
Value: $0.10-0.25

Bakemon

Card #: ST-45
Type: Champion
Value: $0.10-0.25

Mammothmon

Card #: ST-46
Type: Ultimate
Value: $0.10-0.25

WereGarurumon

Card #: ST-47
Type: Ultimate
Value: $0.10-0.25

SkullMeramon

Card #: ST-48
Type: Ultimate
Value: $0.10-0.25

Red Offensive

Card #: ST-49
Type: Force FX
Value: $0.10-0.25

Yellow Offensive

Card #: ST-50
Type: Force FX
Value: $0.10-0.25

Green Offensive

Card #: ST-51
Type: Force FX
Value: $0.10-0.25

Blitz

Card #: ST-52
Type: Power Blast
Value: $0.10-0.25

Metal Attack

Card #: ST-53
Type: Power Blast
Value: $0.10-0.25

Counter Attack

Card #: ST-54
Type: Power Blast
Value: $0.10-0.25

To Champion

Card #: ST-55
Type: Power Blast
Value: $0.10-0.25

Ultra Digivolve

Card #: ST-56
Type: Power Blast
Value: $0.10-0.25

Downgrade

Card #: ST-57
Type: Digivolve
Value: $0.10-0.25

Digi-Duel

Card #: ST-58
Type: Digivolve
Value: $0.10-0.25

Red Digivice

Card #: **ST-59**
Type: **Digivolve**
Value: **$0.10-0.25**

Green & Yellow Digivice

Card #: **ST-60**
Type: **Digivolve**
Value: **$0.10-0.25**

Red & Green Digivice

Card #: **ST-61**
Type: **Digivolve**
Value: **$0.10-0.25**

Yellow Digivice

Card #: **ST-62**
Type: **Digivolve**
Value: **$0.10-0.25**

Digimon **97**

Booster Series I

54-card set
8 cards per pack — 5 commons,
2 uncommons, 1 rare
Booster Pack Price . . . . $2.50-$4
Booster Box Price . . . . $45-$75
Complete Set (54) . . . . $25-$50

Editor's Note: While we received a checklist in time for inclusion in this guide, we were unable to ascertain accurate market pricing for the uncommon/common/rare variations of these cards in time for inclusion. The set's release coincided with the compilation of this information. The complete set price listed here is based on the earliest report and is subject to rapid change.

MetalGreymon (Blue)	BO-01	☐
Devimon	BO-02	☐
Leomon	BO-03	☐
Ogremon	BO-04	☐
Meramon	BO-05	☐
Seadramon	BO-06	☐
Shellmomon	BO-07	☐
ShogunGekomon	BO-08	☐
Shellmon	BO-09	☐
Drimogemon	BO-10	☐
Andromon	BO-11	☐
Monochromon	BO-12	☐
Kuwagamon	BO-13	☐
Mojyamon	BO-14	☐
Gatomon	BO-15	☐
Angewomon	BO-16	☐
Magnadramon	BO-17	☐
Ebidramon	BO-18	☐
Gorillamon	BO-19	☐
Vilemon	BO-20	☐
Minotaurmon	BO-21	☐
LadyDevimon	BO-22	☐
Roachmon	BO-23	☐
Asuramon	BO-24	☐
Snimon	BO-25	☐
Jagamon	BO-26	☐
MetalEtemon	BO-27	☐
Crabmon	BO-28	☐
Syakomon	BO-29	☐
Gesomon	BO-30	☐
MegaSeadramon	BO-31	☐
Scorpiomon	BO-32	☐
Dragomon	BO-33	☐
MarineAngemon	BO-34	☐

MetalSeadramon	BO-35	☐
Tapirmon	BO-36	☐
Pumpkinmon	BO-37	☐
Myotismon	BO-38	☐
Phantomon	BO-39	☐
SkullMammothmon	BO-40	☐
Boltmon	BO-41	☐
Piedmon	BO-42	☐
Fly-Trap (Power Option)	BO-43	☐
Coral Rip (Power Option)	BO-44	☐
Aquatic Attack (Power Option)	BO-45	☐
Fly Away (Power Option)	BO-46	☐
Iron Drill (Power Option)	BO-47	☐
Organic Enhancer (Power Option)	BO-48	☐
Option Eater (Power Option)	BO-49	☐
Power Freeze (Power Option)	BO-50	☐
Even Steven (Power Option)	BO-51	☐
Bomb Dive (Power Option)	BO-52	☐
Digiruption (Power Option)	BO-53	☐
Depth Charge (Power Option)	BO-54	☐

Digimon 99

Booster Series I

54-card set
(Preliminary checklist)

Machinedramon	BO-55	☐
Kokatorimon	BO-56	☐
Etemon	BO-57	☐
Whamon	BO-58	☐
Sukamon	BO-59	☐
Gazimon	BO-60	☐
Elecmon	BO-61	☐
Monzaemon	BO-62	☐
Numemon	BO-63	☐
Mamemon	BO-64	☐
Tyrannomon	BO-65	☐
MetalMamemon	BO-66	☐
Datamon	BO-67	☐
Giromon	BO-68	☐
Megadramon	BO-69	☐
Digitamamon	BO-70	☐
Gizamon	BO-71	☐
Raremon	BO-72	☐
ExTyrannomon	BO-73	☐
Deltamon	BO-74	☐
Tuskmon	BO-75	☐
Myotismon	BO-76	☐
Gatomon	BO-77	☐
Cyclonemon	BO-78	☐
DarkTyrannomon	BO-79	☐
MetalGreymon (orange)	BO-80	☐
Floramon	BO-81	☐
Mushroomon	BO-82	☐
Veedramon	BO-83	☐
Togemon	BO-84	☐
Kiwimon	BO-85	☐
Woodmon	BO-86	☐
RedVegiemon	BO-87	☐
AeroVeedramon	BO-88	☐
Garudamon	BO-89	☐

Blossomon	BO-90	☐
Deramon	BO-91	☐
Cherrymon	BO-92	☐
Garbagemon	BO-93	☐
Phoenixmon	BO-94	☐
Gryphonmon	BO-95	☐
Puppetmon	BO-96	☐
Green Digivice (Power Option)	BO-97	☐
Red/Yellow Digivice (Power Option)	BO-98	☐
Crest Tag (Power Option)	BO-99	☐
Crest of Courage (Power Option)	BO-100	☐
Crest of Reliability (Power Option)	BO-101	☐
Crest of Sincerity (Power Option)	BO-102	☐
Crest of Friendship (Power Option)	BO-103	☐
Black Gears (Power Option)	BO-104	☐
Flood (Power Option)	BO-105	☐
Meat (Power Option)	BO-106	☐
Waterproof (Power Option)	BO-107	☐
Pluck (Power Option)	BO-108	☐

Animated Series Edition

(Trading Cards, Upper Deck)

Base Set (34): $5-8
Digimon Silver Set (34): $25-40
Digimon Silver Singles: $0.75-2
Digimon Silver singles are inserted one per pack
Chosen Kids characters carry slight premium over other Silver cards

Digimon Gold Set (34): $1,200-2,500 (estimated)
Digimon Gold Singles: $75-150
Digimon Gold singles are serial-numbered to 100

Selected Kids
Card #: 1
Value: $0.20-0.50

Ready For Battle! Rookies!
Card #: 2
Value: $0.10-0.20

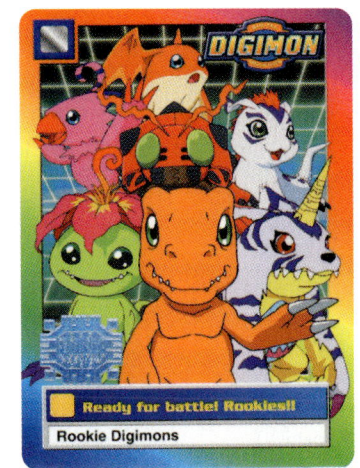

Digivolve! Champions!!
Card #: 3
Value: $0.10-0.20

Tai & Koromon
Card #: 4
Value: $0.20-0.50

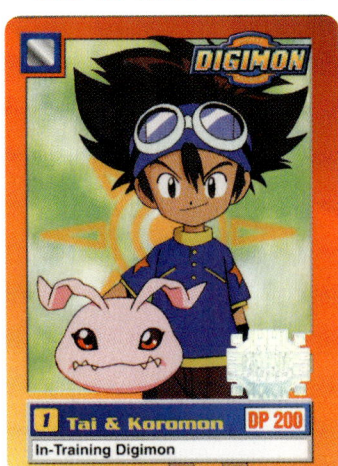

Matt & Tsunomon

Card #: 5
Value: $0.20-0.50

Sora & Yokomon

Card #: 6
Value: $0.20-0.50

Izzy & Motimon

Card #: 7
Value: $0.20-0.50

Mimi & Tanemon

Card #: 8
Value: $0.20-0.50

Joe & Bukamon

Card #: 9
Value: $0.20-0.50

T.K. & Tokomon

Card #: 10
Value: $0.20-0.50

Augumon
Card #: 11
Value: $0.10-0.20

Gabumon
Card #: 12
Value: $0.10-0.20

Biyomon
Card #: 13
Value: $0.10-0.20

Tentomon
Card #: 14
Value: $0.10-0.20

Palmon
Card #: 15
Value: $0.10-0.20

Gomamon
Card #: 16
Value: $0.10-0.20

Patamon

Card #: 17
Value: $0.10-0.20

14 Patamon DP 200
Rookie Digimon

Kuwagamon

Card #: 18
Value: $0.10-0.20

15 Kuwagamon DP 250
Champion Digimon

Greymon

Card #: 19
Value: $0.10-0.20

16 Greymon DP 420
Champion Digimon

Garurumon

Card #: 20
Value: $0.10-0.20

18 Garurumon DP 300
Champion Digimon

Seadramon

Card #: 21
Value: $0.10-0.20

19 Seadramon DP 300
Champion Digimon

Monochromon

Card #: 22
Value: $0.10-0.20

20 Monochromon DP 300
Champion Digimon

Birdramon
Card #: 23
Value: $0.10-0.20

Meramon
Card #: 24
Value: $0.10-0.20

Kabuterimon
Card #: 25
Value: $0.10-0.20

Togemon
Card #: 26
Value: $0.10-0.25

Ikkakumon
Card #: 27
Value: $0.10-0.20

Leomon
Card #: 28
Value: $0.10-0.20

Ogremon

Card #: 29
Value: $0.10-0.20

Devimon

Card #: 30
Value: $0.20-0.50

Frigimon

Card #: 31
Value: $0.20-0.50

Bakemon

Card #: 32
Value: $0.10-0.20

Angemon

Card #: 33
Value: $0.10-0.20

Cockatrimon

Card #: 34
Value: $0.10-0.20

Ultimate Chase Insert cards

(Ultimate Chase inserts are inserted one per 11 packs.)

Set (8): $75-125

Etemon
Card #: U3
Value: $10-16

Piximon
Card #: U5
Value: $10-16

MetalGreymon
Card #: U6
Value: $10-16

MegaKabuterimon
Card #: U8
Value: $10-16

Not Pictured

Andromon
Card #: U1
Value: $ 10-16

Monzaemon
Card #: U2
Value: $ 10-16

SkullGreymon
Card #: U4
Value: $10-16

WereGarurumon
Card #: U7
Value: $10-16

Digi Search

Hey, Digi-fans, what's hiding here? Would you believe it's all seven of the chosen kids plus 14 of their Digimon evolutions? See if you can find all 21 names listed below. Names can run up or down, left or right, or diagonally in any direction.

Agumon	Koromon	Tai Kamiya
Biyomon	Matt Ishida	Tanemon
Bukamon	Mimi Tachikawa	Tentomon
Gabumon	Motimon	TK Takaishi
Gomamon	Palmon	Tokomon
Izzy Izumi	Patamon	Tsunomon
Joe Kido	Sora Takenouchi	Yokomon

```
E M I N O M E N A T A N L P M
T A I K A M I Y A D O N A O S
S N W U T N R M I M H L T O Q
B T B A O N Q H O E M I R L B
Z I T M K J S R N O M A M O G
N Y Y L S I O X N O T B P W R
O O G O T K H E N A U V A I O
M P M T M N T C K K S R T Z N
O B A O U O O E A I S J A Z O
N M R J K M N M F T D N M Y M
U A W O H O O Q U F I O O I O
S E M Z U N Y O N B L M N Z T
T O L C X B M O N U A U I U N
N I H S I A K A T K T G I M E
V I L N O M M U I R T A Z I T
```

Answers on page 112

Digi Toes

Do you know which Digimon these toes belong to?

Answers on page 112

Digimon: _____

Digimon: _____

Digimon: _____

Digimon: _____

Digimon: _____

Digimon: _____

Digimon: _____

Digimon: _____

Digimon: _____

Digimon: _____

Digimon: _____

Digimon: _____

Digimon Name Scramble

Unscramble the letters to spell the Digimon's name.

2. OOBAMNT
_____

1. OMADRONN
_____

3. UKUIODRMNYA
_____

4. NSUOMTK
_____

5. ZOMNMONAE
_____

6. KRONMOO
_____

7. CNOCLMOY
_____

8. MRSADAONE
_____

110 Digimon

Digi play

Answers to Name Scramble

1. ANDROMON
2. BOTAMON
3. YUKIDARUMON
4. TUSKMON
5. MONZAEMON
6. KOROMON
7. CYCLOMON
8. SEADRAMON

Answers to Digi Toes

- Agumon
- Kawagaamon 
- Digitamamon 
- Monochromon 
- Garurumon 
- Shellmon 
- Etemon 
- Piyomon 
- Ogremon 
- Elekimon 
- Gizamon 
- Gajimon 

Answers to Digi Search

```
E M I N O M E N A T A N L P M
T A I K A M I Y A D O N A O S
S N W U T N R M I M H L T O Q
B T B A O N Q H O E M I R L B
Z I T M K J S R N O M A M O G
N Y Y L S I O X N O T B P W R
O O G O T K H E N A U V A I O
M P M T M N T C K K S R T Z N
O B A O U O O E A I S J A Z O
N M R J K M N M F T D N M Y M
U A W O H O O Q U F I O O I O
S E M Z U N Y O N B L M N Z T
T O L C X B M O N U A U I U N
N I H S I A K A T K T G I M E
V I L N O M M U I R T A Z I T
```

Answers to Maze

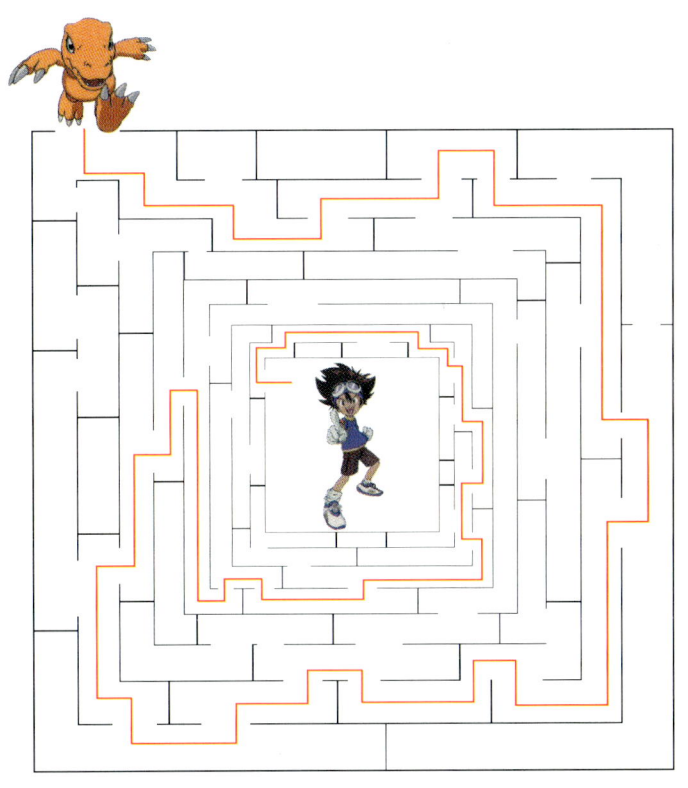

Ad Index

Game Expo	4
Pocket Monsters.com	79
PoJo's Collector Card World	3
PoJo's Pokémon	27

Help Agumon Find Tai!

Agumon and Tai were separated by an evil whirlwind. Help them find each other again as fast as possible. Backtrack if you get stuck in a dead end and remember not to cross over any lines.

Answer on page 112

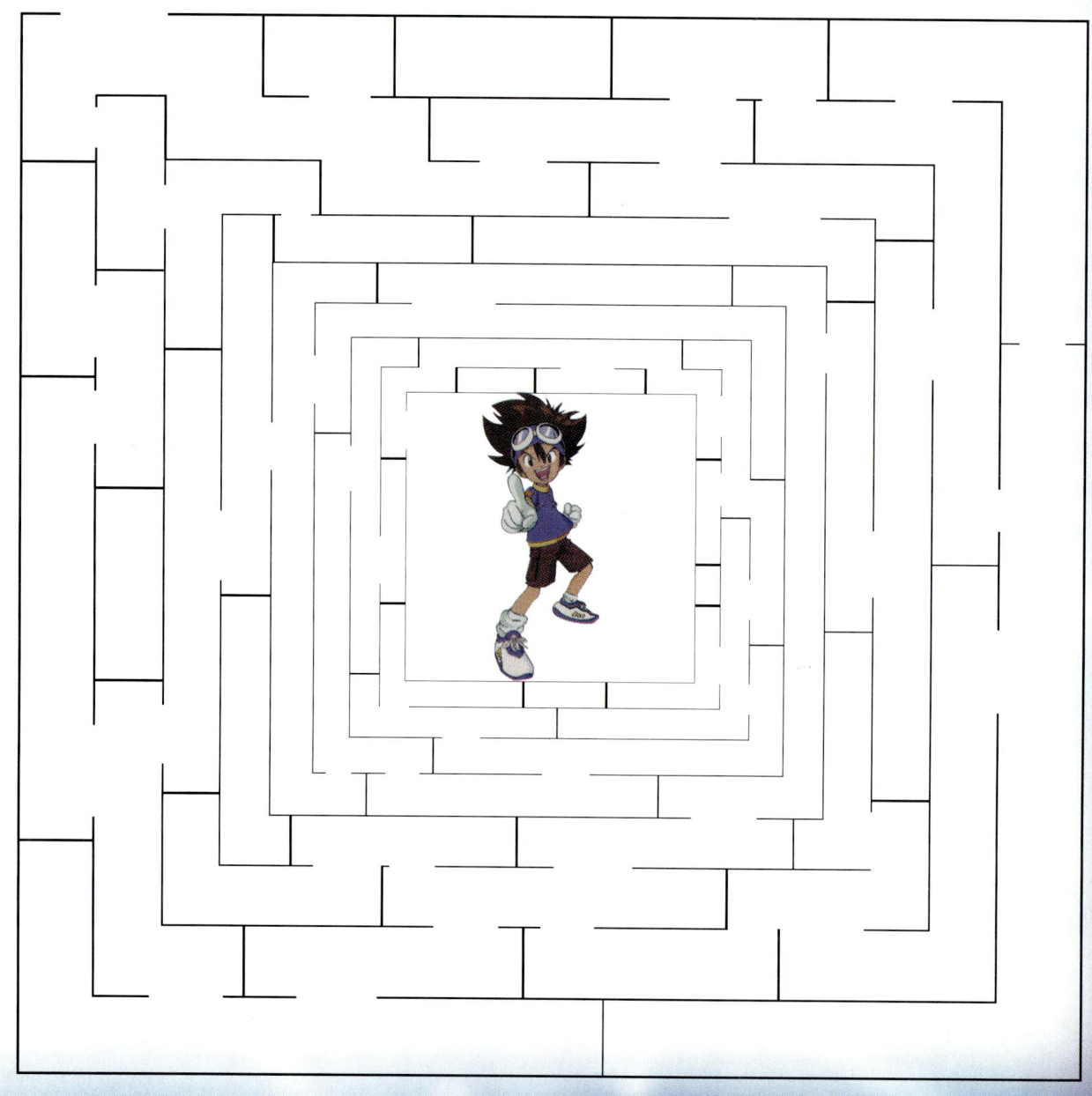